Praise for One Curious Doctor

Hilton Koppe reflects on his life journey, and some of life's most challenging questions, with great clarity, affection, intimacy, and uncompromising honesty. His stories envelop and engage the reader. He takes you into his confidence, allows you into his life, the life of his ancestors, and into the consulting rooms of a country doctor's practice. Hilton's self-reflection and hard-earned wisdom are a gift. Light the fire, settle back in a comfortable chair, and allow yourself to be enchanted.

– Arnold Zable, author of *Café Scheherazade*

What happens when a physician can't simply heal himself? Does he still get to call himself 'doctor' when he no longer sees patients? What is his place in the world? In Hilton Koppe's case, he writes an honest, vulnerable, gorgeous memoir inviting the reader into his journey from illness to health, from his family's origins fleeing Lithuania and Germany during World War II to becoming a country doctor in Australia (via South Africa). Though he no longer works in a clinic, Hilton continues to heal with his words. *One Curious Doctor* is a medical memoir with heart.

– Kim Suhr, author of *Nothing to Lose* and director of *Red Oak Writing*

One Curious Doctor offers the reader an exceptional experience of honesty, vulnerability, insight and transformation. Hilton Koppe, doctor turned patient turned writer, takes us on his momentous journey of a life awakened by the practice of medicine – and the necessity of giving it up. Hilton has listened deeply to the human heart – his patients' and his own. I highly recommend his beautifully crafted memoir.

– Kelly DuMar, author of *girl in tree bark*

One Curious Doctor exposes the reader to the depth and complexities of compassion in healing. It provides insights for patients who are curious about the inner world of their doctors. It is a healing balm for health professionals and anyone impacted by the intergenerational effects of trauma. It gives an ancestral dimension to who we are as humans and who we are as healers. *One Curious Doctor* has universal messages about who we are as compassionate human beings.

– Dr Frank Meumann, GP and Medical Educator

One Curious Doctor gives unprecedented access to the mind of a medical professional as they decide to be kind, no matter the circumstance. You see Hilton Koppe's struggles with the emotional burdens of his work, life, and family history. Then you see him choose, time and time again, to deeply consider the meaning and impact of his words and actions as a doctor.

One Curious Doctor is about his seeking to be kind and empathetic. Hilton chooses to meet his challenges with the pen, firing words and phrases at his doubts until clarity, acceptance, and peace win through. It is a powerful lesson for all of us in how to accept our emotions. And a wise reflection on how creativity, in whatever form, can bring us closer together.

– Professor Catherine Crock AM
Physician, The Royal Children's Hospital, Melbourne
Founder, Hush Foundation and Gathering of Kindness

Wakefield Press

ONE CURIOUS DOCTOR

Hilton Koppe is a writer, workshop facilitator, podcaster and doctor living on Bundjalung land on the east coast of Australia.

A Memoir of Medicine,
Migration and Mortality

ONE CURIOUS DOCTOR

HILTON KOPPE

Wakefield Press

Wakefield Press
16 Rose Street
Mile End
South Australia 5031
www.wakefieldpress.com.au

First published 2022 by Hambone Publishing Melbourne, Australia
This edition published by Wakefield Press 2023

Copyright © Hilton Koppe, 2023

All rights reserved. This book is copyright. Apart from
any fair dealing for the purposes of private study, research,
criticism or review, as permitted under the Copyright Act,
no part may be reproduced without written permission.
Enquiries should be addressed to the publisher.

Every effort has been made to trace and seek permission for
the use of the original source material used within this book.
Where the attempt has been unsuccessful, the publisher
would be pleased to hear from the author/publisher
to rectify any omission.

Revised edition edited by Julia Beaven, Wakefield Press
Typesetting of revised edition by Michael Deves, Wakefield Press
Based on text design by David W. Edelstein
Front cover design by Larch Gallagher
Back cover photo of Hilton by Alana Potts

ISBN 978 1 74305 988 3

 A catalogue record for this book is available from the National Library of Australia

 Wakefield Press thanks Coriole Vineyards for continued support

*For Aliza and Liam
And all future Story Keepers.*

*In memory of my grandparents and parents
Who knew when to leave and where to stay.*

It is not a labour I chose, but rather one for which I was chosen by destiny as I near my journey's end. I regard it, despite all its imperfections, as my masterpiece ... as an effort which is the culmination of a whole life dedicated to the search for truth.

Henri Matisse

CONTENTS

Doctor's Note	xi

HISTORY OF PRESENT ILLNESS
The Sum of the Parts	3

PAST MEDICAL HISTORY
The Medicine of Presence	19
The Making of Me	24
The Red or the Pen	26
Black Dog Stew	32
Remembering John	35
Our First Conversation: Sandra's Story, Part 1	39
Fractured	44
Virtue	46
How Many Patients Can I See in One House Call?	49
Wonderings	53
Dreaming of Viagra	57
Talking to a Dead Man	62
I'm Losing My Patients	66
Final Conversations	68
Mystery	72
Diary of a ~~Wimpy~~ Wounded Doc	80

MEDICAL EDUCATION HISTORY
Eight Seasons: Sandra's Story, Part 2	91
Literary Medicine	97
Making It Real: Sandra's Story, Part 3	103

SOCIAL HISTORY

Imagining My Other Mother	113
Diaspora Boy	116
Slice of Life	121
What If I'd Listened to My Heart?	124
Where Dreams Meet Delusions	131

FAMILY HISTORY

Ignoring Vital Signs	139
Bearing Witness	144
Denial Impossible	147
Duet for the Dead	150
Finding My Family	152
On My Mother's Side	155
On My Father's Side	174

EXAMINATION

Match of the Day	207
Ode to My Stethoscope	213

DIAGNOSIS

Speed Grieving	217

TREATMENT PLAN

After All This	223

PS	230

DOCTOR'S NOTE

Welcome to *One Curious Doctor*. Thank you for your willingness to take over the care of the stories set down in this book.

Some of these stories were born out of my experiences working as a doctor in small-town Australia for over thirty years. Other stories have their roots in my personal journey as a migrant growing up in 1960s Sydney. As a descendent of grandparents who were forced to escape Europe to survive. And as the son of parents who died prematurely from conditions that modern medicine, my professional domain, could not cure.

In 2019, these worlds collided. I was diagnosed with post-traumatic stress disorder. I received this diagnosis both as a shock – *This can't be happening to me. I'm a doctor. Not a patient!* – and as a gift – *Does this mean I actually get to rest now?*

As the fallout from the trauma of the diagnosis began to settle, I tried to work out how I ended up in this position. Was the PTSD a consequence of the repeated losses I experienced in my working life? Did it come from my life-long feelings of being an outsider trying so hard to fit in?

Or was it a result of trauma experienced by my parents and grandparents in their search for security across three continents? And if so, how much of this was learnt, how much inherited?

Maybe it was all down to my personality type. My nature. Did the qualities that made me a trusted doctor also make me more vulnerable to the inevitable impact of caring for people over many years?

I do not yet have answers to these questions. But I am keen to share my ponderings with you in *One Curious Doctor* – the case history of a doctor who is curious to understand more about himself; and who is also curious in the sense of perhaps being a little unusual.

Be patient with this curious doctor. He has done his best without always getting things right. And be patient with yourself. These stories may lead towards an inquisitiveness about your own life. A quest of this nature could unmask uncertainty or discomfort. Sound medical advice would be to reach out for support if this happens.

I have laid out the history for you in the form of a traditional medical record. For non-medical readers, I hope this structure will act as a gentle guide into the world of a doctor.

One Curious Doctor contains stories about some of my former patients. Many have kindly consented to their stories being included. Where I was unable to contact patients or their families, personal details have been changed to maintain their confidentiality.

You may like to begin reading where most medical histories start – the History of the Present Illness. There are footnotes in this section linking to other stories in the book told in greater detail.

From there, follow your instinct. This history need not be read from start to finish. I trust that you will find the most helpful approach for yourself.

All I ask is that you care for these stories as a kind doctor might care for a new patient – with curiosity and compassion.

With my best wishes,
Hilton Koppe, MB BS MFM FRACGP

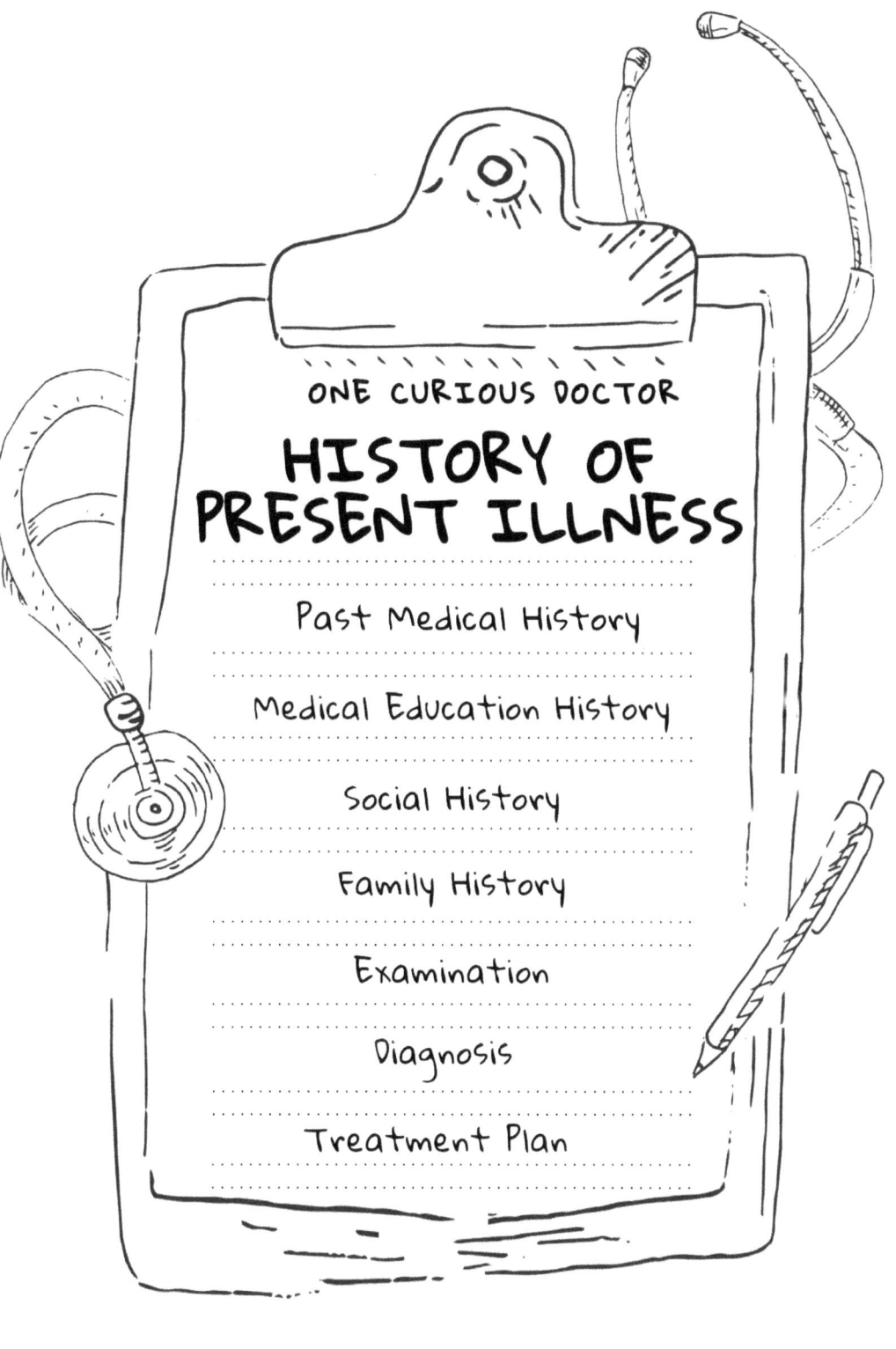

THE SUM OF THE PARTS

My doctor sits back and with calm clarity tells me, 'You're done.'

'Done? What do you mean, done?'

'You've got PTSD. Classic case. An accumulation of forty-something years in medicine. All that vicarious trauma. The only safe solution is to stop work.'

I take this in, the message my body has been trying to give me for months. 'We're one doctor short for a couple of weeks. Can I work until next Friday and then take some time off?'

'No, you're done. You need to make that call.'

Before that ...

My doctor gives me the good news. 'Your brain scan is normal.' Maybe it's the relief that I don't have a brain tumour, but when he asks how I'm feeling, it all comes tumbling out. 'Work is terrible. My patients are so complicated. Three died on me last month. I agonise over who'll be next. They've infected my dreams. I dread going to work. I never used to be like this.'

Before that ...

This is the most at peace I have felt on a work-day morning for ages. I feel safe. No one can get to me here. I'm lying in an MRI scanner. The scanner's drumming reverberates in my head. My eyes jolt open. If this feels peaceful, then I'm in big trouble!

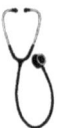

Before that ...
I'm a patient in the emergency ward of the local hospital. Initial tests for a stroke are negative. My symptoms fade with this news.

Before that ...
The right side of my face goes numb in the middle of a challenging conversation with one of my long-term patients.

Before that ...
I'm terrified I'm going to kill someone. I haven't killed anyone in four decades of doctoring. I'd never forgive myself if that happened. I ask the other doctors at the clinic if I can go off the emergency roster. I tell them about my increasing anxiety. My colleagues of the last twenty years decline this request.

Before that ...
Joe is my third patient to die this month. I met Joe while he was still a strong active man. Then dementia hit. The last time I saw him, he looked so much smaller. Lying unresponsive in a nursing home bed can do that to a man.

Before that ...
My neck pain is getting worse. None of the treatments are helping. It wakes me twenty or thirty times a night. When the pain is at its worst, life feels unbearable.

Before that ...
I write lists of what to do to keep my patients alive. Long lists. I wonder if I am becoming obsessive.

Before that ...
My patients have grown old with me. They suffer the indignities of older age with varying degrees of grace. I have kept them alive and now their lives are filled with pain, physical and existential. I don't want to fail them further.

THE SUM OF THE PARTS

Before that ...
I develop chronic neck pain. The cause of the pain is uncertain. I wonder if it might be stress related.

Before that ...
I visit the Jewish Centre of Culture and Information in Vilnius. I spend hours trawling through databases trying to learn about my family. The only information I have to add is my mother's parents' original family names. I search databases of births and deaths and passport applications. Nothing. I look at the marriage listings, scrolling rapidly through hundreds of names without much hope. My eyes catch sight of the names Nisonas Busmanas and Reveke Lurijite. I stop scrolling. *That's them! That's my grandparents!* At the age of sixty, I have learnt the actual names of my grandparents and great-grandparents. When they were born. And where they lived.

Before that ...
I travel to Russia with some of my Lennox Head soccer teammates to watch the World Cup. We are based in Kaliningrad. On a four-day break between matches, we go to Vilnius in neighbouring Lithuania. I want to walk in the footsteps of my mother's unknown ancestors. My mates want to drink beer and visit castles of the Teutonic knights.

Before that ...
I work very hard at practising preventative medicine. I manage my patients' risk factors for heart disease and diabetes. I encourage them to exercise and eat well. I routinely screen them for early signs of cancer. I never know whose life I may have saved by doing all this.

Before that ...
I am selected to play soccer for Australia at the World Cup in Brazil. This is what I tell everyone. It's partly true. I am chosen for the Australian Doctors' team – the Master Docceroos. The World Medical Football Tournament, like a world cup for doctors, is being

played in Brazil during the real World Cup. My first game is against Lithuania. *Ah, an opportunity to play against some long-lost relatives*, I naively think. The Lithuanian men are tough brutal men who have lived tough brutal lives. My thoughts undergo a shocking reframe. *These aren't the descendants of my long-lost relatives. These are the descendants of those who killed my long-lost relatives.* We lose the match.

Before that …
My brother and I sit in the front row at our father's funeral. It's our first time in a synagogue since my brother's bar mitzvah forty years ago. The rabbi gives us the sign. We stand. We struggle our way through the unfamiliar sounds of the Mourner's Kaddish, the traditional Jewish prayer for the dead. A duet for the dead.

Before that …
My father dies from what turns out to be a preventable dementia. I was unable to save his life.

Before that …
I'm invited to Harvard Medical School as Visiting Professor of Medicine and Humanities. It's a long journey from small-town Australian family practice. I share my reflective writing workshop with the students and staff. The goal of the workshop is to deepen empathy and reduce the risk of burnout and compassion fatigue. The workshop and its presenter are well accepted.

Before that …
I love teaching new GPs about the joy of country practice. I share my secret discovery with them. 'Even the most exciting medical conditions eventually become boring, but people are endlessly interesting. If you can find joy in the relationships with your patients, you will have a long and happy career in general practice.'
I realise that the best way to ensure my longevity as a rural doctor is to work part-time in clinical practice and to have other work-related

THE SUM OF THE PARTS

interests that sustain me. I split my working time between my clinic and medical education. This offers a good balance to my working life.

Before that ...
Liz is my last patient before lunch. I see her sitting in the waiting room. She reminds me so much of my mother when she was on treatment for cancer. Liz's results are normal. Her cancer is gone. My mother was not so lucky.

Before that ...
The path from my mother's grave is lined with mourners. Each person shakes my hand and says, 'I wish you a long life.' The wisdom of this tradition ushers me away from death towards life.

Before that ...
I am blessed to be with my mother at the end, her breath transforming from laboured grunting to soft sucking. Until that final explosive sigh. It scared the life out of me, her body relaxing completely for the first time in her life.

Before that ...
I'm with my mother in the waiting room of a clinic treating women with the genetic mutation that causes breast and ovarian cancers. It's a sobering experience sitting among these emaciated Jewish women of Eastern European descent whose fate will be decided by experimental protocols. As if Ashkenazi women did not already have enough to bear.

Before that ...
I begin offering writing workshops for doctors. To help them cope with the emotional impact of their work. The workshops are surprisingly successful.

Before that ...
My mother is perched in the special lounge chair we bought to make her visit more comfortable. She is having her fourth round of

chemotherapy. We are watching the movie *Fiddler on the Roof*. 'You know, Hilton, this story of Tevya and Golda and their *shtetl*, the small Jewish village in Eastern Europe where their family had lived for generations, it's the same as it was for my parents' family,' she confides. This is news to me. No one ever speaks of the traumas that drove my mother's parents to leave Lithuania. Or of those who didn't survive.

Before that ...
I start writing about being a doctor. As my pen gives voice to the unspeakable – despair, grief, fear, betrayal – stories and poems emerge. The writing process is surprisingly helpful.

Before that ...
A patient shares with me poems of her journey through depression. One poem describes me as ignorant, stupid, cruel and naive, offering care less nuanced than an 18th century barber–surgeon.
When my son is old enough to start playing soccer, I realise how much I've missed playing. I join a team of fathers. We dub ourselves 'The Rainbow Sharks' because we are of varied abilities and come from diverse backgrounds. I find a brotherhood among my teammates, which I imagine is similar to the bond between soldiers.

Before that ...
I take six months off work when our daughter is born. The days are long, but the months are short.

Before that ...
We build our family home on the edge of the village. There are photos of my son exploring the building site, which are spitting images of photos of me when my parents built our family home on the outskirts of Sydney forty years earlier.

Before that ...
Our son is born. I never imagined I had capacity for such love. I

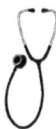

develop empathy for my patients who are parents and a love for their children that at times cripples my decision-making.

Before that …
It's my first Medical Staff Council meeting for over a year. I am struck by how hunched over and serious the other doctors are. Burdened. Worn down. Sitting with them is nothing like sharing a campfire with fellow travellers.

Before that …
My wife and I spend a year travelling around Australia. I do a couple of locum stints in Western Australia. Each week of work supports a month of life on the road. We spend most of our time camping in national parks and share campfires with people from all walks of life. I feel energised and alive.

Before that …
I tell my patients of our plans to travel around Australia. One of my older patients says to me with tears in his eyes, 'Good on you, Hilton, I always wanted to do that. But I don't suppose I'll get the chance now.' My colleagues are not quite as supportive.

Before that …
I'm barefoot and shirtless as I walk the track to Angourie Point. I pause and rest the palm of my left hand upon the gnarly bark of a banksia. I feel the tree's wisdom as it helps me make a life-changing decision. *Yes, you can leave your patients. They will be okay without you. Yes, it's okay to follow your dream. Do it while you still can. Life is short and precious.*

Before that …
I miss a diagnosis of appendicitis in a young boy. I misinterpret crucial signs because I'm preoccupied with resentment at having to do a home visit when I think his mother should have brought him to the clinic. Word of my mistake quickly spreads around town.

Before that ...
From the waiting room at the clinic, I overhear a conversation between one of my older patients and three-year-old Ruby. Ruby tells the older woman that she is coming to see me because she knows that I love her. Hearing this makes my day.

Before that ...
At our garden wedding, Sharon walks down a path with a parent on each arm. At the same time, I walk down a separate path with a parent on each arm. Where the paths meet, Sharon and I link arms and walk forward to the *chuppah,* the Jewish wedding canopy. The miracle of crossed paths. Sharon's family has lived in this region for generations. My family is one of Holocaust survivors. And yet, here we all are. Raising our glasses. Sharing a traditional Jewish toast, '*L'chiam*! To life!'

Before that ...
In my dream, I see my mother in a flowing white gown. She's dancing through the trees. Free. Unburdened. Playful. She turns toward me. Despite everything, her expression says, *Don't worry, I'm going to be fine.*

Before that ...
I walk home from the clinic for lunch. I'm expecting a call from my mother. She is getting the results of her breast biopsy. The bad news comes as I am getting changed out of my work clothes.

Before that ...
It's the morning of 29 February 1992. As we lie in bed, Sharon turns to me and asks, 'Will you marry me?' It's the easiest question I've ever had to answer. 'YES! YES! YES!' The clairvoyant was right!

Before that ...
I'm introduced to Sharon on a Friday night at the Railway Hotel in Byron Bay. She sits at the opposite end of a long table. In the middle of much noisy conversation I try to impress her by doing

THE SUM OF THE PARTS

impersonations of a local bloke who channels The Archangel Michael. A quintessentially Byron way to commence a courtship.

Before that ...
Living and working as a GP in a small town is rewarding and challenging. There is a quiet joy that comes from doing home visits to 100-year-old farms where extended families still live together.

Before that ...
I buy my first house. For the first time since leaving school, I am able to live in the same house and work in the same job for six consecutive months.

Before that ...
It takes time to be accepted as the new GP in Bangalow. I try not to take it personally when patients tell me that their previous doctor used to do things differently.

Before that ...
I'm shocked and a little embarrassed when my mother bursts into tears as I drive off. I'm leaving Sydney to be a country doctor. The last time I saw Mum cry like this was twenty years earlier when she'd said goodbye to her parents after we'd visited them in South Africa.

Before that ...
For my thirtieth birthday, I throw myself a Lack of Commitment party. Guests need to answer four questions:
Are you married?
Do you have a child?
Do you own your own home?
Do you own your own business?
If anyone answers *Yes* to more than one of these questions, they must show cause as to why they should be allowed to come to a Lack of Commitment party. I am proud to answer *No* to all four questions.

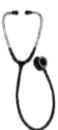

Before that ...
On the long drive home to Sydney from Brisbane Expo, I stop off in Byron Bay to go to the toilet. I've heard stories of Byron's magical qualities. This is my first visit. It's a stunning October day. The woman in the ice cream shop tells me how good life has been since moving here from the city. 'Sounds great! You don't happen to know of a job for a doctor in town, do you?' I ask her jokingly. Her reply is barely audible. 'The doctor in Bangalow, a village just inland from here, was killed in a car accident last week.'

Before that ...
The practice I am working for in Sydney offers me a partnership. This would be a huge commitment for me. I tell them I will think about it while I am on my upcoming road trip north.

Before that ...
I'm unlucky in love. I consult a clairvoyant. Her prescription is simple. 'If you want to find a woman who loves being by the sea and under the trees, then you must go and live by the sea and under the trees.'

Before that ...
I'm sent to Coffs Harbour for my rural GP training placement. Within a week, I've met four generations of women from one family. I can care for my patients at the local hospital. For the first time since entering medicine, I know what I want to do.

Before that ...
After all the anguish and anxiety of being a medical student, the experience of working as a hospital resident is overwhelmingly underwhelming. I place an advertisement in a medical newspaper. *Disillusioned doctor requires mentally stimulating job with normal hours. Will hear any offers. Dr Hilton Koppe, Hornsby Hospital.* The only response I get is from the hospital's medical superintendent. I'm summonsed to his office. Perhaps he might be concerned that one of

THE SUM OF THE PARTS

his doctors is suffering. But all Dr Heinrich says is 'Don't you dare use our hospital name in public like that ever again!'

Before that ...
Teaching-hospital ward rounds are daunting. I trail at the end of a hierarchy that extends from the specialist at the summit, down the slope of red-caped charge nurses, behind long-white-coated residents and blue-capped trainee nurses into the valley of short-white-coated medical students, where I cower in fear of being asked a question. Somewhere in the shadows lies the patient. As we leave the bedside, I whisper to the patient, 'Don't worry, I'll come back later and explain to you what all that means.' I'm puzzled by the origins of my newfound empathy.

Before that ...
As a medical student, I am no longer the misfit I was in high school. I am with a bunch of misfits. For the first time in my life, I feel like I belong. Which makes the suicide of one of my classmates all the more distressing.

Before that ...
I'm sitting alone with my mum in our lounge room after my first day of second year medical school. She rests her hand on the back of mine as my personal world is shattered. 'Dad is leaving us. He's found another woman.'

Before that ...
At medical school, I struggle academically. Organic chemistry is a mystery. Anatomy is another language. Formaldehyde gives me headaches. If I fail first year, I'll have to find something else to study.

Before that ...
I scrape into medical school by a few marks. My entry grade for English Literature is ninety per cent. My previous best was sixty-nine per cent. Essays on Kenneth Slessor's poem *Five Bells* and Shakespeare's *Hamlet* sneak me into medicine. This makes my parents happier than I've seen them in years.

Before that ...
At high school, I'm proficient academically but lack career direction. My parents send me to a psychologist. He concludes I should study medicine if I get the grades. I wonder if he's aware of my father's and his father's foiled dreams of being a doctor.

Before that ...
I am a sullen adolescent. I dream of playing soccer for Australia. Perhaps that might be my escape.

Before that ...
I am not cool enough for the cool kids. I am not brainy enough for the brainy kids. But I am different enough for a beating.

Before that ...
At thirteen, I go through bar mitzvah. My parents honour this promise to my mother's parents who remained in South Africa. I nervously wipe my sweaty palms on my suit pants as I wait to be called to the *bimah*, the raised platform in the synagogue. My father attempts reassurance by putting his arm around my shoulders. 'You'll be all right,' he says. This is the only memory I have of physical affection from my father.

Before that ...
My family doesn't celebrate Christmas. Mercifully, my birthday is on 24 December. When the other kids ask what I got for Christmas, I list my birthday presents.

Before that ...
My mother takes my brother and me to South Africa to visit her family. I wonder if my grandparents will have black skin because they live in Africa. When we arrive, my mother asks the porter to take our bags. I'm perplexed. 'Mum, why did you just call that man boy?'

THE SUM OF THE PARTS

Before that ...
I have salted tongue or pickled herrings on my school sandwiches, not ham or Vegemite. In the summer holidays, my classmates spend time with their cousins and aunties and uncles. My only two cousins live in South Africa. I've never met them. I feel the shame of being different.

Before that ...
My father refuses to continue to live under the increasing oppression of South Africa's apartheid regime. He is aware of what his parents endured to give their family a life of freedom. The decision is made to move to Australia. Many South African Jews have made this journey. My mother's family is either unwilling or unable to take the journey with my father's family. I am two years old when we migrate. My brother is nine months.

Before that ...
My father visits Bloemfontein on a business trip from Johannesburg. A matchmaker introduces him to my mother. He is twenty-four. She is nineteen. They marry the following year. My mother leaves her family and moves to Johannesburg.

Before that ...
My father studies medicine for a year at Wits University in Johannesburg. He is not cut out for academic life, despite his father's urgings and shattered dreams. He leaves university for a life in commerce.

Before that ...
My father's family find refuge in Paris for a few years before fleeing the menace of Nazi Germany. My father's mother has an uncle who lives in South Africa. He is a doctor and an owner of racehorses. He sponsors the family to move to South Africa. And saves their lives. That's what doctors are supposed to do.

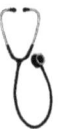

Before that ...
My mother's parents settle in Bloemfontein and live a simple life among the Jewish community. They rent a small apartment in the ostentatiously named Hilton Mansions. My mother is born there.

Before that ...
My mother's father convinces my grandmother to leave their *shtetl* in rural Lithuania for a better life in South Africa. Many Lithuanian Jews have made this journey. Their families are unwilling or unable to take the journey with them. My grandparents never see any of their relatives again. The Germans and the Russians make sure of this.

Before that ...
My father's father is arrested by the Gestapo after refusing to be bribed by one of his employees. My grandmother goes to the police station where he's being held. The arresting officer is their neighbour's son. My grandmother reminds the young Nazi that they helped his family during The Depression. As he uncuffs my grandfather, he whispers to my grandparents, 'You can go. But you must leave Germany. Tonight. Never come back. I won't be able to help you next time.' My grandparents and their two sons catch the night train to Brussels. My father is two years old. My uncle is nine months.

Before that ...
My father's father dreams of becoming a doctor. His dream is snuffed out by chronic dysentery, a souvenir from the trenches of Eastern Europe, and by The Depression.

Before that ...
My mother's father is conscripted into the Russian army. My father's father is conscripted into the German army. They are enemies during World War 1.
Thankfully they were not good shots.
Or I might not be here telling you this story.

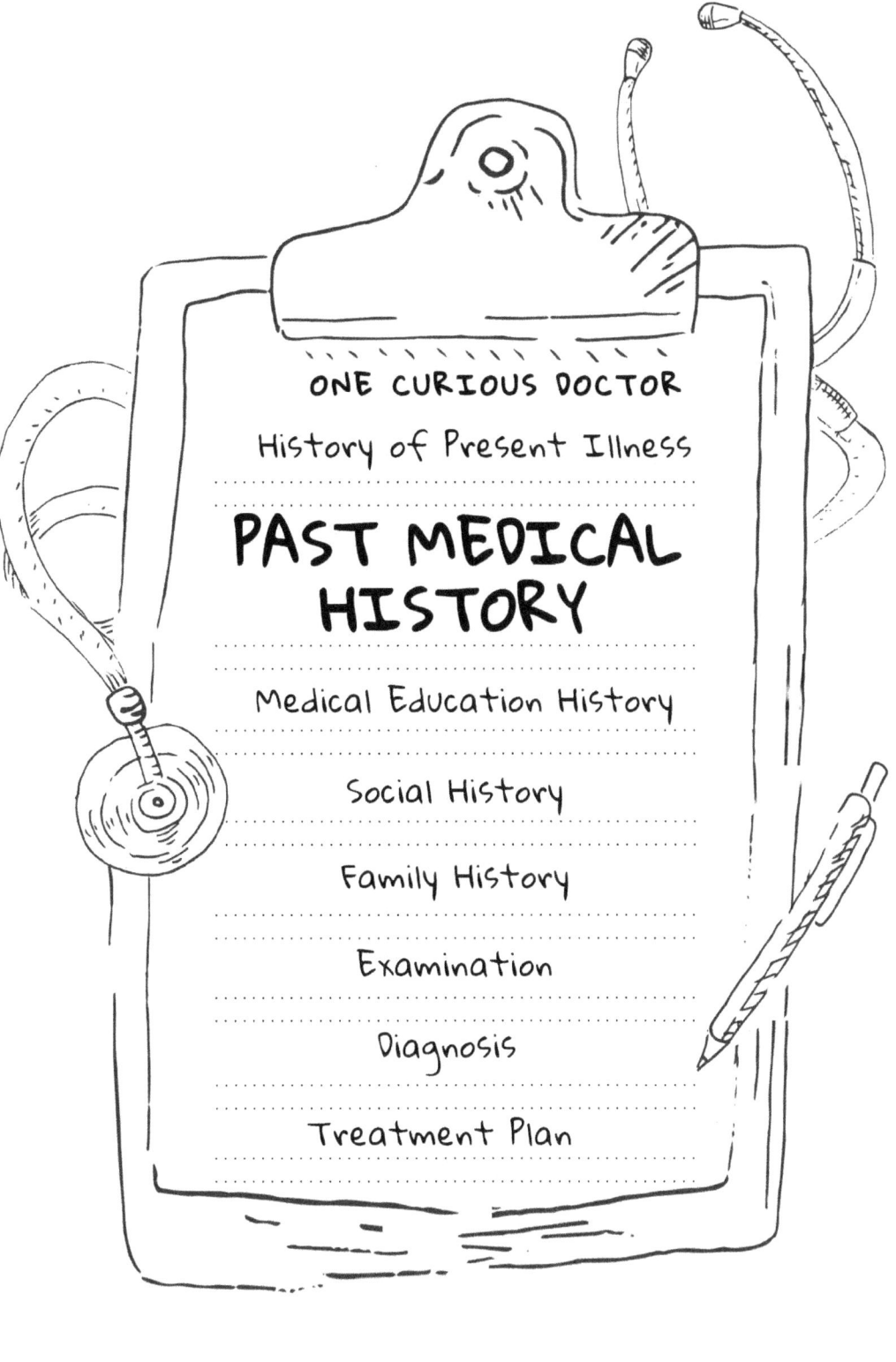

THE MEDICINE OF PRESENCE

It took longer than expected to be accepted as the town's new doctor. I was very different to the previous doctor. Younger. 'An ethnic', as those of my ilk were called. Xenophobia was alive and kicking in rural Australia in the 1980s.

The town's children were the first to welcome me. They weren't bothered by my unpronounceable name or foreign features. They cared that I cared. That was the pulse they took in assessing my trustworthiness.

The children's acceptance of me led their parents to take some hesitant steps in a similar direction. I'd notice the wonder on a parent's face as their hyperactive son sat quietly while I looked in his ears. Or when their shy young daughter engaged confidently in conversation with me. *He must be doing something right*, their expression told me.

On a busy Monday morning, I overheard three-year-old Ruby talking with one of my older patients in the waiting room. I had been present at Ruby's birth. 'Why have you come to see Hilton today?' the old woman asked. 'I've come to see Hilton because he loves me.' Not *because I'm sick*. Or *because I want him to make me better*. But *because he loves me*.

I used to do the childhood vaccinations. There was no practice nurse in those days. I offered the kids choices during the vaccination process. To help them feel they had an element of control. Even if they didn't get the choice to refuse the needle.

'Where would you like to sit when you get your needle? On the bed? On the chair? Or in your mum's lap?'

'When we're finished, what sort of Band-Aid would you like? Dorothy the Dinosaur? Spiderman? Or Thomas the Tank Engine?'

'Which arm would you like the needle in? Your right arm?' as I gently touched their right shoulder, 'Or the left?'

'When you feel a sting from the needle, say *ouch* as loud as you can.'

Using this approach, things usually went pretty well. One time, a five-year-old girl turned as she was leaving my room after getting two needles and ran back in, giving me a quick kiss on the back of my hand before rushing off with her mother.

In time, the rest of the community came to trust me with their medical care. I believe that my commitment to being fully present with the person in front of me might have started that process.

My lifelong sense of unworthiness as an outsider made it difficult for me to recognise this acceptance. I had to teach myself how to detect my patients' confidence in my care and their gratitude for it. It wasn't always immediately apparent. The reticence of working-class Australians is profound.

I gradually learnt to see things more clearly. When a new patient told me that one of their friends had recommended coming to my practice, or when one of my adult patients brought an aging parent to see me, I told myself that those actions were their way of showing gratitude and trust. I wasn't inundated with Christmas gifts or garden produce as I once imagined would happen for a country doctor. But I could sense a growing ease from my patients as we sat in each other's presence.

As the decades have gone by, the relationships with my patients have deepened. Experience has taught me to be more patient. Less judgemental. I have become less of a tradesman or handyman and more of a confidant. One of my patients started calling me Sigmund (as in Freud). Another, Father (as in Confessor, the irony of which was not lost on this Jewish doctor).

THE MEDICINE OF PRESENCE

More often now, I am able to notice when my patients might say, 'Thanks for listening, Hilton.' Or, 'Thanks for being there for me.' Or, 'Thanks for helping me get through that.'

Ben was my last patient for the day. He came back to review his asthma. I had noticed a suspicious-looking mole on his back a couple of weeks earlier while listening to his lungs with my stethoscope and suggested he see a skin cancer doctor to get it checked.

'The specialist said you were absolutely right to send me along,' he said. 'It was a melanoma. He reckoned we got it just in time. Thanks for being so thorough. Most other doctors I see listen to my chest through my shirt. Pretty hard to diagnose a melanoma that way.'

It's difficult to know how best to respond to my patients' gratitude. In a way, I'm just doing my job. But the relationship between a patient and their doctor can be more than merely a transactional, 'You tell me your problems. I'll do my best to solve them. Please pay on the way out'. I have invested a little of myself in them, as they have trusted in me.

I guess my response to their gratitude would usually be an automatic, 'You're welcome,' or, 'It's a pleasure.' Kind of like the mindless 'Good thanks, and you?' response to being asked, 'How're you doing?'

As I get closer to the end of my career, I have begun to wonder if perhaps there could be a deeper truth underlying my seemingly mindless replies to receiving thanks from my patients. Do these phrases give voice to unspoken feelings I have for my patients? Maybe these feelings are unspoken because uttering them might be interpreted as being unprofessional. Too familiar. An enactment of the forbidden trespass across the patient–doctor boundary.

The reality is my patients *are* welcome. I invite them into my room as I might a guest into our home. I share my mind and heart with them. The duality of being focused and open at the same time. Focused thinking as my brain works overtime problem-solving on their behalf. An opening of my heart as I bear witness to their joy or suffering.

And, it is a pleasure. Surely it must be human nature, an evolutionary advantage, to experience pleasure in easing the suffering of another. I've found it a privilege to spend time in the service of my patients. My own pain drops away as I sit in their presence, creating a safe and healing space for them. I sometimes wonder who gains the most benefit from these interactions.

As a family doctor, my greatest joy comes from assisting people at the end of their lives. 'Enjoys palliative care' might not be the best advertisement, but it is the part of my clinical practice that offers the most meaning. So much of modern medicine feels like swimming against a rip. End-of-life care is different. It allows me to float on an incoming tide. To work with Nature, not to fight against Her.

Being with a person at the end of their life also gives me the opportunity to care for them in their home. When they are no longer able to visit me at the clinic, I put time aside to visit them. The gratification that comes from being welcomed into people's homes is magnified by my past. It is a light that illuminates the shadow of growing up as a migrant. Of being the descendent of Holocaust survivors. Of having grandparents who were identified as enemy aliens after leaving Europe.

I am grateful to my adopted community. They trusted me to be a midwife to death at the end of their lives. People like Ted and his family, who welcomed me into their lives at the end of Ted's life.

Ted was the father of a friend of mine. He had spent the previous four months in a city hospital having treatment for leukaemia. Much of this time had been spent in isolation while he had no functioning bone marrow.

Ted wanted to come home to die. He didn't want any more invasive life- prolonging treatments. His daughter asked if I would be able to care for him once he was discharged, as his previous family doctor did not make house calls. I was delighted to accept the invitation.

I met Ted for the first time at his home on a Tuesday afternoon. His wife, son and two daughters were there, along with hordes of grandchildren. The energy in the house changed and a hush fell with

THE MEDICINE OF PRESENCE

the announcement, 'The doctor's here!' There is still a mysterious magic when a doctor arrives for a house call.

I was shown into Ted's bedroom. He was sitting up in bed reading the sports section of the paper. My initial impressions were that Ted was a no-nonsense sort of guy, one who appeared to have been in control of most things in his life. The sort of bloke who tolerated incompetence poorly. I liked him instantly.

This first visit was a time for me to get to know Ted and his wife. And for them to get to know me. So that we could develop a shared understanding of the care he would want in the coming days.

During my daily home visits, I tried to assess where things were up to and to prepare Ted and his family for what I thought might happen next. Everyone knew that Ted was dying. My job was to walk with Ted and his family along this unmapped path with as few unexpected bumps as possible.

Ted's progress was quite straightforward. He died peacefully in his home ten days after we met. Although his family was thrust from being carers into the hands of grief when Ted died, they were relieved that it was the death he had wanted.

His daughter hugged me and whispered through her tears, 'What a privilege to have been with Dad in his final days in such a close way. Thanks for making that happen.' His son, a knock-about sort of bloke so much like his father, offered his gratitude with a gnarly hand on my shoulder. 'Thanks so much, Hilton, that was awesome. Well, no. Not awesome. Terrible. Sad. Terribly sad. But somehow perfect at the same time.'

I acknowledged their thanks through stifled tears with a barely audible, 'You're welcome. It's a pleasure.'

THE MAKING OF ME

I was the new doc in a small country town. I wanted to be accepted. I wanted to be respected. I tried so hard to do the best I could for all my new patients.

She was the town matriarch. She had multiple chronic illnesses. She had the power to make me or break me. I had suggested that she see a specialist in the city. I wanted to make sure she was on the right treatment. I didn't know the specialist. I hoped that he would treat her well. I wanted his care to represent an extension of my care.

She came back to see me after the visit to the city, still on the same treatment. I was keen to know how the specialist had treated her. I asked her about this. She said that he was the best doctor she had ever seen. I asked her why.

She gazed down at her hands. Pensive. Silent. She gently cupped her right hand in her left. She then slowly ran her left thumb over the tips of the fingers of her right hand, appearing to be in a trance. She finally spoke, as she continued to explore her own hands as if for the first time.

'Before he sounded my heart … he … he took my hands in his … and he … he just looked at my hands … for a really long time … It was amazing.'

I was mesmerised.

For the last thirty years, her story comes back to me as I pause to look at my patients' hands before I examine the rest of their body.

THE MAKING OF ME

I stand by the side of this person lying on my examination couch. I give them my full attention. I take their hands in mine. I look at their hands closely. In silence. Slowly. Respectfully. Intentionally. Methodically.

Every day, I am reminded of the matriarch's teaching of the sanctity in this moment of commune. To pause and connect prior to further laying on of hands. I learn so much about my patients as we share this quiet moment. I wonder what they learn about me.

I am grateful to the town matriarch. She may have been the making of me.

THE RED OR THE PEN

*The poems flow from the hand unbidden
And the hidden source is the watchful heart*

Derek Mahon, 'Everything is Going to be All Right'

It was late. I was alone; the rest of my family was in bed. I was tired, but happy. I reached for a glass of wine. Reward for completion of my accounts for another month. And there they were. The pile of poems. In the bottom of my in-tray. Unread.

They had been sitting there for how long – three months, six months, nine months? Too many poems. Too thick a pile. Too scary. I was intimidated by the weight of the words. Intimidated, yet curious. I reached for the pile. Poems of a journey through illness and recovery.

The poems had been written by a patient. Not just any patient. The patient who had caused me the greatest anguish in my twenty years of family practice. Depression, despair, desolation – we had shared those experiences for months. A year, perhaps. Patient and doctor. Sufferer and sufferee.

None of the treatments I suggested worked. Antidepressants made her worse. They stopped her feeling. And when she couldn't feel, she couldn't write. And when she couldn't write, she couldn't see the point in living. How can a poet live without writing?

The psychologist was too mechanical. The CBT was boring and predictable. The psychiatrist kept putting up the drug doses.

THE RED OR THE PEN

Nothing worked.

It was late. I was alone. And there they were. The pile of poems, on the table. I reached for them.

'The Tractor Poems' was typed on the front page. *What does that mean? Something to do with ploughing? With the turning of the earth? I don't know. I'm no good at this poetry stuff.*

Below the title, a handwritten note in red ink. 'Remember, poetry can be a fiction too. Happy reading. S.' And a simple smiling face. Two dots above a dash above a curved line. The smiley face disturbed me.

What does that mean? That you are happy now? That you are going to get the last laugh? Might it be better to let sleeping dogs lie?

She had written the poems during her recovery. No, she had written the poems *as* her recovery. Once she had stopped taking the drugs and started to feel. Once she stopped doing what everyone else suggested. Once she stopped trying to be a good patient. Stopped pretending. She started to write again. And she started to get better.

It was late. I was alone. And there they were. The pile of poems. In my hands.

I flicked through them. The titles made no sense. 'Cricket', 'To the Headland', 'Test Test Testing', 'God Is a Potter'. She had told me the poems were about her illness. I couldn't recognise illness anywhere in these.

And there it was, towards the bottom of the pile. 'And You', it was called.

Could that You be referring to me?

I was not so different to other doctors. I wanted my patients to like me. No, I wanted my patients to love me. To think that I am a great doctor. To appreciate my desire to help. My desire to heal.

So what did 'And You' have to say about me? I expected to read about how I had been the one to make the difference. The knight in shining armour. That without me, she would not have got better. That I had been the one, the only one, who had been there for her through all the blackness.

I scanned the poem, too scared to dive right in. Then I saw

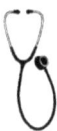

the letters ECT and knew what this poem was going to be about.

It was going to be about the darkest hour of our journey together. None of the treatments were working. She refused to see anyone else. I didn't know what else to do. I felt alone. Responsible.

From out of this black hole came a clutching offer. 'I'm not sure if you are aware of it, but in cases of severe depression like yours, when no other treatments help, ECT, or shock treatment, is sometimes still used. It can be very effective.'

In all my years of medical practice, I had never before needed to utter those words. As they catapulted from the depths of my desperation into the space between us, two images flooded my mind. The padded cell in the lock-up section of the local psych ward, which I had visited when I had first arrived in town. 'Just wanted to check out the local facilities,' I had mumbled to the medical superintendent, as the horror of the cell was etched into my memory.

And at medical school, during my psychiatry term, going with my newly admitted patient for her first shock treatment, her terrified face etched into my heart.

'ECT, or shock treatment, is sometimes still used. It can be very effective.' How would my patient react to those words. What would she think? It was hard to tell. She was still being a good patient.

'And You' was about to let me know.

And You

These are the things that I could have been before you knew me,
(please tick which boxes apply):
☐ restaurateur
☐ mother
☐ recruitment consultant
☐ Avon lady
☐ travel writer
☐ fuckwit
but now I'm not.
And you,

THE RED OR THE PEN

who knows nothing,
sit there and say:
If not
☐ hospital then perhaps
☐ ECT.
There's always ECT.
I'll just put it out there.
You say.
And I say to you:
Sylviajanetvirginiaernest
and more.
You look abashed or possibly bored
though more likely you are just
a gentleman of science revealing
your ignorance
your stupidity
your naivety
your cruelty
to suggest violence
(incredible)
to cure pain.
And I say to myself:
Black dog's girlfriend is little kitty heroin.
I should perhaps instead seek a vet.

It was late. I was alone. Everyone else in my family was in bed. The poems were no longer in a pile on the bottom of the tray. They were scattered in front of me. The lid was off Pandora's box.

And you? And you! What about me? What about all this emotion? All this anger, this resentment, this hurt, this shame! What am I supposed to do now? How am I to respond?

My first thought, *another glass of wine*. It had always helped in the past. But it felt too late for that. And there they were. This pile of emotions. Too much for a glass of wine.

My next thought, *to write a poem*. Write a poem in response. To be understood. To be heard.

No one ever hears the doctor's story. Bloody patient-centred medicine. I practise it. I teach it. But what about us? What about me? We are not inert punching bags, there to accept without judgement all that is thrown our way. Bugger it, there are two people in this doctor–patient relationship, and I am one of them. If it's good enough for her to write a poem about me, even though I'm no good at this poetry stuff, I'll give it a go.

To be with, or to do to? That is the question.

A start shamelessly stolen from my old mate William, and from my own consulting skills workshop. A tentative start. A gradual increase in momentum. I found words pouring directly from my heart, brain bypassed. As the words flowed, so did the tears. Unexpected. Uninvited. But welcome. Relieving.

Just keep writing. Just keep writing. Don't think. Just write.

And I did. I wrote, and I felt better.

A Physician's Lament

To be with
Or to do to
That is the question.
To do no harm by being with
An other
Separate, yet not
Different, yet not
Flesh and blood, both.

But what when being with is not enough,
When being with only
Does harm?
When there is a need to do to

THE RED OR THE PEN

To do to
And to do no harm.
Now there is a question
To vex the mind body spirit
Of this flesh and blood.

Where is the wisdom?
Where is the wisdom I need?
To whom can I turn when my
mind body spirit flesh blood flounders,
When my inner well is dry,
Except to the thoughts of others,
Past and present
Who have trodden similar paths before me
Or for me
So that I may
Be
and
Do
For You.

Time, they say, heals all wounds. But sometimes, time alone is not enough. For me, as for her, it was writing that triggered my healing. Another shared journey.

Now, when it is late, when I am all alone, when the rest of my family is in bed, I write. Just a little each night. A few more poems. Some short stories. The making of a play.

I don't care if I'm no good at this poetry stuff, if my writing is crap, because now I feel better too.

BLACK DOG STEW

Some of my colleagues don't believe in evidence-based guidelines. They say it diminishes the art of medicine. Turns it into a cookbook. 'You can train a monkey to follow a recipe.'

Me, I find comfort in knowing there are researchers who have applied proven scientific methods and given deep thought to which treatments work best.

But in some respects, my doubting colleagues are right. Many patients in my country practice have conditions for which there are no guidelines. Research is usually done on people under 75 years of age with only one medical condition. I have very few patients like that. Even when my patients do fit the guidelines, the recommendations don't suit everyone.

In times like these, I need to make up my own recipe and hope it turns out okay.

The story of my patient who had written a poem comparing my care to that of a vet continued to haunt me. While the initial poem I'd written in response to hers helped in the moment, it felt incomplete.

So I reached for the pen again. Like last time, the words flew onto the page. But this time, I was less frantic. I sat with the words longer. Played with them. I tried to engage the imaginative part of my brain. To put my emotions to one side and just have fun with what was on the page in front of me. To make up my own recipe.

A Slow-Cooked Black-Dog Stew for Two

Required Equipment

Deep cast-iron pot

Pot-stirring implement

Sharpened cleaver

Electric blowtorch

Ingredients

Patient – freshly crushed

Black Dog – untameable

Quart of muddy water

Doctor – overripe, bruised

Psychologist – green

Psychiatrist – non-malleable

Employer organisation

Multinational insurer

Tablespoon of acrimony

Dash of fermented adversarial style

Psychologist – red

Method

1. Blend patient with black dog to form paste with consistency of melted tar
2. Slosh muddy water into deep pot
3. Immerse paste in muddy waters over maximum heat until drowning point is reached
4. Add doctor, psychiatrist and green psychologist. Stir hopefully
5. Reduce heat and simmer until all flesh falling from bones
6. Finely dice employer, insurer, acrimony, and adversarial style

7. Chuck diced mixture into pot from great height
8. Continue to simmer for nine months until all ingredients thoroughly reduced
9. Sprinkle over red psychologist to form an optimistic crust
10. Threaten to blacken crust with electric blowtorch
11. Let sit
12. Hope for the best

I put down the pen. Took a breath. Re-read the poem. Reflected on how I was feeling in that moment.

This isn't too bad! And it was fun. Maybe I can do this poetry stuff.

I wondered if writing in this way might diminish the impact of the worrying and repeated losses encountered in my work? And what about my colleagues who face similar situations? Might they too be helped in this way?

Perhaps a new guideline on the therapeutic benefits of poetry and reflective writing needs to be added to medicine's cookbook.

What harm could one more recipe do?

REMEMBERING JOHN

I remember you the day we met. I was scared shitless. You were relaxed and at peace, as always. For me, it was my first soccer game for twenty-five years. For you, it was just the start of another season, your loping languid style belying your skill and speed.

I remember you sitting next to me on the drive home from a game at Nimbin. Telling me about your long journey with Crohn's disease. About needing to have your large bowel removed ten years earlier as a result of intractable symptoms. About your two broken bones last year. I couldn't stop myself from being a doctor. 'Men in their thirties shouldn't have fractures from minimal trauma.' I suggested you get your bone density checked. Was it okay for me to do this? I was your friend, not your doctor.

I remember you asking me to be your doctor. You said that I had cared enough, while driving home from a soccer game, to recommend looking deeper into your medical situation. That a willingness to look deeper was a quality you craved in a doctor.

I remember you sitting in my clinic room. Many years of shared conversations. Me, offering ideas. You, running your race, in your own way. Not always by the book. But always with great intelligence and equanimity.

I remember you telling me that you were moving 1500 kilometres south to be with your newfound love and soon-to-be mother of your child. You were so happy, and I was so happy for you.

I remember you getting cancer a few months after your daughter was born. An aggressive bowel cancer. I heard it from Mick. Your brother. My friend and teammate. I was devastated.

I remember you moving back to our hometown to have more treatment after your surgery. You were so positive despite the rough road you were travelling. It was not so easy for me to be optimistic. I did my best, despite what my medical training taught me about your likely outcome.

I remember you disappearing into the abyss of the hospital system. I used to get letters from medical oncologists and radiation oncologists and surgeons. I didn't see you for a while. My thoughts were with you during this time.

I remember bumping into you at night while I was out walking our dog. You preferred being outside in the cool of the evening. I enjoyed our late-night conversations. It was hard to see for sure in the shadows of the sparse streetlights, but you didn't look well. Side effects of the treatment, perhaps?

I remember you coming back to see me at work after your chemotherapy and radiotherapy had finished. We agreed to work together to try to prove the gloomy specialists wrong with their poor predictions. Now I could see for sure that you didn't look well. The result of fourteen months of treatment, you said.

I remember you telling me about the lump in your neck. I could not ignore it, as much as I wanted to. It was hard for me to remain positive when the likely outcome was catastrophic. You implored me to be honest with you. To tell you everything I knew. You said you would rather get news from me, no matter what it was.

I remember meeting you at your front door when I pulled up on my bicycle the day after you had the lump biopsied. 'I hope you're not the bearer of bad tidings,' you said. Unfortunately, I was.

I remember you sitting at your kitchen table with your wife and your baby daughter, trying to comprehend the incomprehensible. It was the only time I saw you cry.

I remember you thanking me for coming. 'It's so much better to

get these results from you here at our kitchen table than what it would be from the oncologist in his office tomorrow. At least I'll be better prepared for what he has to tell me now.'

I remember you deciding to have one more go at chemotherapy. An attempt to ease the discomfort you were feeling. You knew there was no cure. But you weren't ready to die. Not yet.

I remember you carrying your daughter down the beach. Even though you'd only had to push the pram a few hundred metres from your home, you looked exhausted.

I remember you deciding to stop the chemo. It wasn't helping. You were getting sicker. You didn't want to spend any more time in hospital.

I remember you vomiting mercilessly. Not being able to eat or drink. Getting weaker.

I remember you asking me if I could look after things so you could stay at home. I gave you my word that I would do whatever I could to honour your wish.

I remember visiting you the last time I saw you out of your bedroom. You were on the floor with your daughter playing dress-ups. She confidently fitted you with angel's wings as if they were the most natural thing in the world.

I remember us speaking about how quickly things were deteriorating. I said, 'If there's anything you want to do, best do it soon.' You got married the next day.

I remember you beaming as you showed me your wedding ring. You were so happy, and so sick.

I remember you looking like you would die in the next few days. I told you what I thought. You thanked me. You said that it was a relief to know that the end was coming.

I remember you telling me what a great job your wife and sister and brother were doing in caring for you. How having such a good team made your job easy. We both knew what your job was.

I remember you speaking with me for the last time. You told me how fantastic it was having your face wiped with a frozen cloth. 'Like

duck-diving through a wave at The Point,' you said, with a smile on your face.

I remember you being quiet and comfortable. As the medication did its magic. Allowing me to honour my promise to you.

I remember you at peace shortly after you died. Your wife and daughter and brother and sister and father with you. I was so proud of you. Of a life well lived and a life well died. I cried tears of sadness at your loss, and tears of joy that your suffering was over.

I remember you for your courage and openness, your wisdom and determination, your spirit and love. It was a privilege to have known you. It was an honour to have cared for you.

I remember you, John.

OUR FIRST CONVERSATION
SANDRA'S STORY, PART 1

I knew about Sandra before I met her. Kev, one of my soccer teammates, is a nurse at the local cancer care unit. At training one Tuesday evening, he told me about Sandra. She had just returned to our small town, having spent the last six months with her four-year-old daughter Tahlia at a teaching hospital in the city. Tahlia was being treated for leukaemia and was now on maintenance treatment. They had come home. Sandra needed a family doctor to co-ordinate Tahlia's care. Kev thought that Sandra might benefit from some emotional support. He knew I was interested in supporting people facing serious illness and thought I would be a good person for her to see.

Part of me felt honoured that a friend who knows me warts-and-all, like soccer teammates do, would suggest that a patient under his care might benefit from my medical attention. Part of me felt anxious about what I might have to offer. I wondered how traumatised Sandra might be after such a life-challenging experience. I wondered how I might cope with adding another traumatised patient to my list. And part of me felt annoyed that work had intruded into one of my refuges. A place where I wanted to be Hilton. Not Dr Koppe. Just for an hour or so. *Is that too much to ask?*

A week later, Sandra turned up at my clinic. She came alone, armed with a thick lever-arch folder. I guessed that the folder contained key documents from her daughter's medical history.

This was daunting – how was I expected to digest this huge pile of information? And a relief – the hospital in the city had not yet sent medical notes to my practice.

Fortunately, Sandra knew enough about the medical system to make a long appointment. I welcomed her into my room and invited her to share her story. I didn't tell her that Kev had told me that she might come. I wanted Sandra to feel that I was starting our conversation without preconceptions.

Sandra shared the story of her family's journey with leukaemia. She told me about Tahlia's diagnosis. 'Tahlia presented with irritable mood and complained of sore legs,' she began. 'At first, they thought she had growing pains. But then she refused to walk, and a lump developed under her left eye. They organised a scan. And that's how the leukaemia was found.'

She continued, telling me about the treatments. The battles with side-effects. She told me about her efforts to get what was best for Tahlia. About where the medical system had done well. And about where it had let them down.

It sounded like a well-rehearsed story, I thought. One that had been told many times. It was told with distance, as if Sandra was a passive observer of the story. Not one of its central characters. I guessed that this was a survival strategy. Parents of children with serious illness get very good at it. Very quickly. To protect their children from their own horror.

But on this occasion, Tahlia was not present to hear the story. So, I made an offering to Sandra. Something like, 'You don't have to pretend when you come in here. Or hold it all together. I'd like this room to be a sanctuary for you. A place where it's okay to let your guard down. If you ever need to. I'd like to think that there is nothing you could tell me which I wouldn't be able to hear.'

Sandra leant back in her chair, her gaze upward and to the left, as she scanned her mind. Which folder to reach for in her memory bank. First, there was silence. Then, as she looked out the window beyond the confines of my room, tears began to appear. The floodgates opened.

OUR FIRST CONVERSATION

'It's pretty weird being home again after six months living out of a suitcase', she sobbed. 'I spent most of that time with Tahlia at the hospital. My husband and other daughter stayed at home. They came up some weekends. I felt bad most of the time. Like I wasn't doing enough for Tahlia, even though I was there every step of her journey. I couldn't protect her from the trauma of all those things they did to her. To make things even worse, I felt like a terrible mother to my other daughter and a hopeless wife. Like I'd abandoned half my family.'

This is better. Tears are a good sign. Now we're getting somewhere.

Without averting my eyes from Sandra's, I reached for the tissue box from the shelf above my desk and placed it on the small table beside her. This display of compassion was superfluous. Sandra was well prepared with her own supply of tissues.

As if on cue, Sandra's tears stopped. My silence encouraged her to continue.

'The hospital staff were amazing at their job, but you have to tell the same story over and over and over again, and no one ever asked how I was. I'm a psychologist. I understand the trauma of being the parent of a critically ill child. They thought Tahlia was going to die when she was first diagnosed. It's a miracle we're still here, but no one asked how I was coping.'

I remained silent. Legs uncrossed. Feet flat on the floor. Hands resting in my lap. Soft gaze. Listening with every cell in my body.

'And now we've got to deal with the side effects from the drugs Tahlia's on. She doesn't even look like our daughter anymore, with all the weight she's put on. And no hair. She gets these wild rages. It's like she's possessed or something. There's nothing I can do to calm her down. Tantrums are bad enough in a two-year-old, but now she's six, it's a nightmare.'

In that moment, my mind flashed to a scene that I'd witnessed a few days before. A bald bloated girl on the backseat of a car screaming for her life as she scratched at her mother's face. Tahlia!

This memory flicked a switch. I was no longer present with Sandra. Images exploded across the wide screen of my mind's eye.

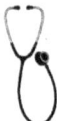

I saw Tahlia. Fighting.

For her life.

She was the same age as my daughter. I could see my daughter in Tahlia's situation. Fighting.

For her life.

Not my little girl!

Sandra's fear. Her pain. Her suffering. They had just become my fear, my pain, my suffering.

I started to cry. To cry!

In the middle of a conversation with a new patient, who I had just told could share anything.

What a fuck up. What a total fuck up. The doctor is supposed to be there to support the patient. Not the other way round. I managed to quickly swallow my tears. But I was embarrassed. And ashamed.

'Sorry, sorry, sorry,' I blubbered as I turned and reached for the tissue box. 'It's not fair that you have to watch me carrying on in such an unprofessional way. After everything you've been through.'

I had really wanted to help Sandra and I felt like I had failed. I doubted I would see her again. Surely she would want to find a real doctor. A doctor who could hold their shit together. I doubted that Sandra would have been confronted by doctors in the hospital who let their guard down in the way I had. What is it about my personality that makes it so hard for me to separate my feelings from my professional persona?

I saw Kev at training the following week. I can't remember who started the conversation. I'd like to think it might have been Kev. 'Sandra really appreciated seeing you. She said it was such a relief to finally find a human doctor.'

But it might have been me who brought work onto the soccer field this time. 'I think I stuffed up with Sandra. When she was telling the story about Tahlia, I started imagining our daughter in her situation and I lost it. Big time.'

OUR FIRST CONVERSATION

Kev looked away. 'Maybe we should go and warm up with the other guys, hey?'

Despite me being convinced that I'd failed her, Sandra did come back to see me the following week. She has continued to visit me regularly. Sandra has brought along Tahlia. And her little sister. And Tahlia's father and grandparents. They all see me now.

Maybe I was being a real doctor all along?

FRACTURED

Mr WS – 40 years old
New patient.
Rock wall builder.
No significant past medical history.
Sent in by ex-wife to discuss 22-year-old son's medical condition.

> *I see the dreams of*
> *this fractured man*
> *sitting in front of me.*
> *Dreams he held for his son.*
> *As a father myself*
> *these unbidden visions*
> *are a distraction from*
> *my role as a doctor.*

Consent previously given by son for me to share general overview of case only.
Clear instructions not to discuss specifics of symptoms or treatments.

> *I see his dreams.*
> *They are familiar dreams.*
> *A father's dreams for his first son.*
> *Dreams of his son growing up to be happy and healthy.*

FRACTURED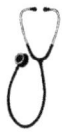

> *Dreams of them sharing activities and experiences together.*
> *Dreams of being more engaged with his son*
> *than his father had been with him.*
> *Happy dreams.*
> *Hopeful dreams.*
> *Solid dreams.*

General information shared.
Directed to relevant websites.

> *I see his current dreams.*
> *Dreams of his son initiating a conversation.*
> *Dreams of his son having meaningful relationships.*
> *Dreams of his son holding down a job.*
> *Troubled dreams.*
> *Doubtful dreams.*
> *Lonely dreams.*

Questions answered without revealing details of son's case.
Offered further discussions as needed.

> *As we part*
> *he offers me thanks*
> *and his calloused hand.*
> *In my mind we trade places.*
> *How would I cope if my son*
> *were in his son's position?*
> *Dreams have been fractured.*
> *Minds have been fractured.*
> *Lives have been fractured.*
> *Schizophrenia does that.*

VIRTUE

Some days general practice can be tough going. Too many insoluble problems. Not enough time to deal with things thoroughly. It's on days like these that I try to find joy or meaning in the midst of the slog. It's an effort but, with practice, finding joy or meaning has become easier. Almost habitual even.

Like last Monday.

It was one of those typical Mondays in the middle of flu season. I was just managing to keep my head above water when one of our receptionists asked if I could squeeze in a father and his daughter. 'They said they needed to be seen this morning, and they asked specifically to see you, Hilton.'

I was not the Duty Doctor for the day, so technically I didn't have to see them. But if I didn't someone else would have to, so I agreed, begrudgingly, to fit them in at the end of the morning session.

Six-year-old Chloe and her dad Paul had been to see me a few times before, as had other members of their family. Perhaps they thought of me as 'their doctor'.

I particularly enjoyed seeing Chloe. She's an outspoken young person in a refreshingly honest way. I imagined that this honesty and enthusiasm for life may pose some challenges for her at school and socially, so I wanted her to know that I was genuinely interested in what she had to say.

By the time I came to see Chloe and Paul it was clear I was not going to get a proper lunch break, so I decided to do what one of my

VIRTUE

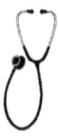

mentors taught me early in my career. 'When running late, just go slow. Don't rush to catch up. It's impossible.'

It seemed clear early on that both Chloe and Paul had a mild form of the virus going around, and there were going to be no significant clinical challenges for them. So I decided to channel the wisdom of my mentor. I slowed down and relaxed into the joy this visit may offer.

While I was examining Chloe, I asked her a question I often ask my patients, with varying responses. Some people struggle to come up with an answer, but I was confident that Chloe's would be enlightening.

Hilton: *I haven't seen you for a while Chloe. Tell me something good that's happened in your life recently.*
Chloe: *Dad said that I could go to Catholic scripture at school so I can do my first Holy Communion.*

I was surprised by the content of her answer, but not that Chloe would have something interesting to say. Paul looked surprised too, as parents often are when their children feel confident to give an honest response to a question of this nature.

The conversation continued.

Paul: *I don't remember saying that.*
Chloe: *Yeah, you know, after Grandma said I should do Catholic scripture instead of Ba'hi scripture, you said I could do it. Grandma said I need to do Catholic scripture so that I can do my first Holy Communion.*
Paul, to me: *Grandma is pretty keen on the religious stuff.*

I could sense a little family tension, which needed some diffusing.

Hilton: *Ba'hi scripture must be pretty interesting. I bet they teach you great stories in Ba'hi scripture.*
Chloe: *Yeah, a few good stories, but mostly they just talk about virtues.*
Hilton: *Virtues, now there's a fantastic thing to learn about at school. I wish I'd learnt about virtues when I was at school. Tell me about your favourite virtue.*

Chloe: *Well, I have two favourite virtues. Love and compassion.*
Hilton: *Love and compassion. What great virtues. How do you practise love and compassion?*
Chloe: *I practise love and compassion every day by giving my mum and my dad a hug and telling them that I love them.*
Hilton: *And when you practise your virtues of love and compassion in that way, how do your mum and dad react?*
Chloe: *They like it.*
Hilton: *How can you tell they like it?*
Chloe: *Well, I can see on their faces that it makes them really happy.*
Hilton: *And how does that make you feel?*
Chloe: *It makes me really happy too.*
Hilton: *It sounds to me that it's a pretty good thing to practise your virtues, because it not only makes the people around you happy, but it makes you happy too. Is that right?*
Chloe: *Yeah, that's right.*
Hilton: *You're so lucky to be learning about virtues at school.*
Chloe: *Yeah, I am!*

By this point in the conversation, I didn't know for sure how Chloe and Paul were feeling, but I was feeling a whole lot better than I had been ten minutes earlier. I suspect they both felt a little better too.

And isn't that what a doctor is supposed to do?

HOW MANY PATIENTS CAN I SEE IN ONE HOUSE CALL?

I'd been dreading this moment for weeks. I knew it was coming. But I didn't expect it would come so soon. Ever since Greta had invited me to be her doctor, I knew all roads were leading to this point.

Greta had ovarian cancer. Like my mum, Greta had been treated with surgery and chemotherapy. Like my mum, Greta's treatment held her cancer at bay for a time. Like my mum, Greta's cancer came back.

There were other similarities too. Their gentle nature. Their love for family. Their uncomplaining acceptance of their fate. Their generous smile. Their fair complexion. Their rotund shape. Their European heritage.

Greta had asked me to take over her medical care because she wanted a doctor who was experienced in caring for people at the end of their life. I wondered if she knew how deeply my experience actually ran.

I was aware that caring for Greta would bring back memories of my mother's illness and eventual death. I tried to be mindful of seeing Greta's journey as uniquely hers. Not as a replay of Mum's. This dance was not easy. The dance between the past and the present. Between imagination and reality.

As Greta's cancer advanced and she decided to have no further chemotherapy, the parallels became alarming. I hoped that being conscious of the similarities would not hinder my ability to care for Greta. That perhaps it might help to make me more compassionate.

But I worried about my emotional response to her journey and how to manage the clash of the present circumstances with past experience. Not just with my mum. With multitudes of patients. Visions of my journeys with them jarred like a cracked record with the needle stuck in a groove.

And then the moment arrived. The first home visit. The moment that always heralds the beginning of the end. Greta's condition was deteriorating. She was no longer well enough to visit me at my clinic.

As I drove to Greta's home, I sensed Mum's presence. She was by my side, encouraging me as she always did, reminding me to focus. When I pulled up in Greta's driveway, I needed to leave Mum in the car. So I could be present for Greta. I struggled to do this.

Alice met me at the front door. She worked for Home Care, helping those who need extra assistance because of illness or infirmity. Alice had cared for many of my patients. She is an angel. She was also a patient of mine. There, floating above Alice, was a vision of her husband Don. He had been a patient of mine too. Before he died from an aggressive cancer, a few months earlier, at the age of forty-eight. Don gave me a reassuring smile, an encouraging thumbs-up and then vanished as I entered Greta's home.

I was not expecting to meet Alice at Greta's place. I wondered how it was for her, being in the home of someone dying from cancer so soon after her husband had died in a similar way. Her pained expression answered this question. I hoped that she could sense the empathy in my eyes as we shared an unspoken conversation. As I held her in her pain. And moved on to see Greta.

Alice called out to Greta and her partner, 'The doctor's here.' These magical words returned me to my first visit to Ted's house, a house filled with the noise of children and grandchildren, and the hush that fell with the uttering of the spell that announced the doctor's arrival. The kids ushered outside. The in-laws retreating to the kitchen. A similar reverence now fell over Greta's home.

Greta was in bed. She told me how uncomfortable the fluid build-up in her abdomen was becoming. I examined her distended belly. I could feel the tumours growing where she'd had fluid drained

HOW MANY PATIENTS CAN I SEE IN ONE HOUSE CALL?

a few weeks earlier. And I was back with Mum again. In her doctor's room. As he examined her distended belly and told her that he could feel tumours growing where she'd had fluid drained a few weeks earlier. Her doctor had been amazing. He had shown her such respect and always given her his complete attention, no matter how busy he was. I now needed to give Greta my complete attention too.

I could tell that Greta was entering the terminal phase of her life. She needed to go back to hospital to have more fluid drained from her abdomen. I told her what I thought. 'It will only be for a day or two, and then you'll be home again.'

I'd offered the same forced optimism to Bob a few years earlier. When the cancer in his spine was causing so much pain that he couldn't get out of bed. But he didn't come home a few days later. He died on the medical ward. A terrible death. After becoming paraplegic. His wife shared with me her distress that Bob had spent his final days delirious from too much medication. That he had been treated like a number rather than a person. I wanted to avoid a similar outcome for Greta, so arranged for her to be admitted to the palliative care ward where I knew she would get optimal care.

Bob's death in hospital had robbed me of an opportunity to say goodbye; on leaving Greta's bedside, I panicked that I might not see her again. As I turned to the door of her room, I had a vision of Jason in my clinic office.

Jason had metastatic melanoma. He'd had tumours removed from his liver and his adrenal gland, and from his brain on three occasions. Now he had a large tumour in his lung. I was watching a replay of our last conversation before surgery to remove the lung. As we spoke, I had a terrible premonition that he would die on the operating table. I had never experienced anything like that before. It frightened and confused me. Should I tell him? I chose to keep my fears to myself. I didn't have the language to express such an insane idea to a patient. Jason survived the surgery and has fully recovered. Jason reminded me once again that premonitions and visions can be unreliable. Best to focus on the here and now.

Greta's partner accompanied me to the front door, asking me the questions so common at this stage of a terminal illness. 'How much longer does she have? What will happen from here? What more can I do?' I answered the questions as best I could, as I had for Kim's parents and Ted's wife and Thelma's husband and Kevin's children.

I retreated from these impossible questions and spectral hauntings to the sanctity of my car. Waiting there for me was Mum. Quietly sitting in the passenger seat. Reassuring in her acknowledgement of what I had done.

Any vestiges of solitude were shattered when reflections of Reggy and Tina flashed upon the rear-view mirror. 'You never fucking came to visit me at my home,' sneered Reggy from the back seat. 'Or me. Fuck you!' said Tina.

Reggy and Tina were two of my more colourful patients. I had looked after Reggy for years. He had died unexpectedly. In his lounge chair. With a whiskey by his side. Just as he would have wanted. 'I did come to visit you, mate,' I retorted. But it was after he had died. To sign his death certificate.

'And, Tina, what did you expect from me? I saw you weekly for months to keep you going as your cancer ran rampant. You can't blame me for your sudden death from a massive haemorrhage. Give me a break, will you.'

Then they were gone. All of them. Leaving me alone. Completely alone. To battle on. A simple bloke. Who sometimes finds himself in the most complex situations.

WONDERINGS

I have found myself wondering why you didn't tell me you were a singer in a rock-and-roll band. In Liverpool. Liverpool, England. In the 1960s. What a time that must have been. I had to find out from your brother-in-law. In his eulogy. At your funeral. Too late to ask you about it then.

I have found myself wondering what else there was about your life that I didn't know. I thought we knew each other quite well. Did you know that I had seen you more times than any other of my patients? That you were my most frequent flyer. But, despite all those conversations we shared, I didn't know you were a singer in a rock-and-roll band.

I have found myself wondering why your Advance Care Directive was sitting on your dining-room table. On top of all your papers. Was it left there as a gift for me when I came to your home to certify your death? I did feel a little better when I read that you wanted to be allowed to die a natural death. That you didn't want more medical interventions. God knows, you'd had enough of those already. That you wanted to be allowed to die in your home. Best to be careful what you wish for, mate! Cos your wish sure as hell came true.

I have found myself wondering about your last few moments alive. Did you feel it coming? Was there pain? Did the defibrillator in your

pacemaker keep firing off to try to get your heart going again? Did you have time to be scared? Or was it over before you knew what was happening? At least you died in your favourite chair with a glass of your favourite whiskey by your side. Give me that death any day over a failed resuscitation in hospital.

I have found myself wondering what got you in the end. There were so many other ways you could have died earlier. You should have been dead already. Didn't your heart specialist in Sydney say you wouldn't last two years when you moved to the country? Well, we proved him wrong. You got a decade. Even with the buggered heart. And the failing kidneys. And the out-of-control diabetes. And the ulcerative colitis. And the bowel cancer. And its secondaries. As if you didn't already have enough to deal with. I reckon it was the chemo that did it. You ended up in hospital the last two times after chemo. Don't the oncologists know when to stop? But you seemed keen to keep going with it. Still had reason to live. I just hope it was the chemo that got you. Not the high potassium level we found in your blood test that we did a couple of days ago. Cos high potassium is treatable. Easier to treat in hospital than at home. But treatable anyway. I hope it wasn't the potassium.

I have found myself wondering if I killed you by not making you go to hospital like the specialist suggested. Maybe I didn't believe that the high potassium would get you. It had been much higher in the past. And you'd survived. You had the defibrillating pacemaker to shock your heart if it went off kilter. You had the treatment to lower the potassium at home. Surely you were safe. And I couldn't have made the risk much plainer. 'If you don't go to hospital, you could die at home.' Your reply was just as plain. 'I don't give a rat's. I'm not going back to fucking hospital. You can carry me out in a coffin for all I care. I'm not going back to hospital. I've got the treatment I need. I'll take what I've got at home. Stuff 'em. I'm not going to spend what time I've got left in a fucking hospital.'

WONDERINGS

I have found myself wondering about the conversations we shared about what the future held for you. Were they helpful? I knew what was coming. I wanted to guide you along that path. They were difficult conversations. I appreciated your acceptance of my honesty. As upsetting as it was for us both. But no other bastard in the health system was going to tell you. We had already been through so much together. It was the least I could do. You got your will sorted. You patched up your differences with your daughter. You even found a home for your cats. You needed to know the truth.

I have found myself wondering what kept you going the last few years. After your wife died. After all the time you spent caring for her. Watching her disintegrate before your eyes. After having your large bowel cut out. The leaking colostomy bags. Colostomy bags you had to wear after surgery for a cancer you should never have got. After waiting too long for the colonoscopy you were scheduled to have to pick up changes in your bowel before they became cancerous. After having to see all those medical people – cardiologists, gastroenterologists, nephrologists, bowel surgeons, ear surgeons, stoma therapists, diabetic educators, dietitians. You had a nickname for each of them. Perhaps that's what kept you going. Your sense of humour. And your ability to see that people were genuinely trying to help you. Despite the failings within the health system.

I have found myself wondering if I could have done more to get you that colonoscopy earlier. Before your inflammatory bowel disease, which had been well controlled for so many years, turned into bowel cancer. I did the referral when it was due. I didn't know the public system waiting time would be so long. If I did, I would have encouraged you to go private. Or helped you to conjure up some symptoms to bump you up the waiting list. The retrospectoscope makes it seem so easy. But you needed a colonoscope and you didn't get it in time.

I have found myself wondering who I am going to be able to swear with at work now. Who else is going to respond to my innocent question, 'How's things?' with 'I'm fucked and far from home, mate,' as you used to do. And who is going to joke around with me? Like when I suggested you schedule your next appointment earlier than usual to check on your progress, you would say, 'Running short of funds for a new car, are we?' We were a pretty good team. You offered me your humour. I shared my medical knowledge. I reckon I got a good deal!

I have found myself wondering who else is going to call me Hilti. No one but you calls me Hilti. You are a tough act to follow.

And I have found myself wondering whether writing this piece will allow me to bury my loss along with your coffin. To let you go. To say goodbye. To say I'll miss you. And to say thanks for everything you shared with me.

DREAMING OF VIAGRA

I know that it's professionally undesirable. That it can lead to problems. I know that I'm supposed to guard against this. But sometimes, it happens.

I do have favourite patients!

Jock was one of these favourites. Jock and his wife Flo moved to our small community from Western Australia. They had migrated to Australia as Ten Pound Poms during the 1950s. Jock was typical of his generation from Northern England. Uncomplaining and practical. He was in his mid-sixties when I first met him. He suffered from chronic heart disease and widespread arthritis. Years working as a bricklayer meant he was covered in sunspots and skin cancers. Despite his ailments, he was energetic and enthusiastic about life. He loved playing bowls. He was a mad-keen English football fan. Wolverhampton Wanderers was his team.

Jock's health deteriorated. His memory became poor. Unless Flo was with him, he might forget the reason for his appointment. Jock's mother had died from Alzheimer's, and he despaired that he was on the same path. Over time, his heart weakened. He got an infection in his hip replacement that required a prolonged stay in hospital and months of antibiotics. He developed a blood cancer. Then came severe leg pain as a result of a pinched nerve in his spine.

Jock remained stoic and uncomplaining. His main concern was

the pressure he was putting on Flo. He wanted their life to go back to normal. They shared an intimate relationship. He worried his impotence meant he was failing as a husband.

I was struck by the way Jock managed his suffering. His equanimity in the face of growing pain and disability. Our conversations were often as much about football as they were about his symptoms, perhaps to help us both avoid talking about what the future may hold. I wished there was more I could do to ease his suffering.

Writing has been the tool I've used to help manage my emotional response to the suffering I've witnessed in the people I care for. Could writing ease the load I was carrying on Jock's behalf?

I had recently discovered a form of poetry called 'found poems'. Words are taken from an existing piece of writing and rearranged and reshaped. It is like collage with words. I was keen to give this a try with Jock, so I printed his entire electronic medical record. All the visit notes, X-ray and scan reports, letters to and from specialists. The whole damn catastrophe. I took this litany home and spread it over the lounge-room floor. Armed with a highlighter pen and a pair of scissors, I set about trying to find key words, which I could extract and reassemble into something meaningful.

What I discovered was that the words from the medical record were dull. Seriously dull. Even using the found poem approach, they had no literary merit. The best I could create would have been fit for nothing more than a medical meeting.

If I were going to truly honour Jock's journey and my part in it, I would need a more playful approach. I changed the medical jargon into images from nursery rhymes. What a contrast! Now I had something fun to work with. From the shards of Jock's decimated medical record, 'Dreaming of Viagra' was born.

At a visit shortly after completing the poem, when Jock's pain was at its peak, I told him that I had written a piece about his suffering. I was too embarrassed to recite the poem, but did tell him why I wrote it. I shared the poem's title and its final line.

DREAMING OF VIAGRA

On hearing this story, a solitary tear rolled down Jock's cheek, 'Hilton, I always knew you cared about me. I just never knew you cared that much.' This was the only time I saw him cry.

Jock died unexpectedly a few weeks later. It had been a risk telling him about my response to his suffering. He was the patient. I was the doctor. But I was glad that he could hear that I too was dreaming of a Viagra.

Dreaming of Viagra

When you first invited me to be your doctor
You already had
Blocked drains in your heart
And
Two bionic hips.

Not bad for a retired Pommy brickie
With a love for football.

Pretty soon you had
Saggy baggy eyes,
Faulty bionics,
Lost marble memory,
Sprouting barnacles,
Huffing and puffing, big bad wolfing, heart failure,
Flopsy dropsy phallus,
Chaotic blood corpuscles
And
A Humpty Dumpty femur fracture.

All the king's men tried to
Make your bright eyes tight,
Collect your marbles,
Freeze scrape cut burn your barnacles,
Build a house of bricks for your heart,
Stand to attention downstairs,
Poison your blood back to normal,

Replace your broken bionics with new
But
The king's men failed to wipe their boots before entering the cathedral of your hip
Allowing an alien invasion of your new joint.
So
You had to trade your palace for a hospital bed.
No wonder you were down in the humpty dumps.

And now
After years of bloody battle
A strangler fig in your spine
Chokes the nerves to your good leg.

Still,
I try to make you smile
And you oblige
To make me feel better.
But your eyes betray your swallowed cries,
'I want to be able to make love to my wife.'
'I want to be able to play bowls.'
'I don't want to be a burden.'
While
I dream of a Viagra to cure my impotence in easing your suffering.

A few months after Jock died, I was invited to speak on national radio about my journey with writing and how it had helped me as a doctor. I wanted to use Jock's story as an example of the difference that writing had made in my life. To demonstrate how writing helped me to build a deeper connection with Jock. How it helped ease my suffering. How sharing a little of my writing with Jock may have helped to ease his suffering too.

Before I could speak about Jock on national radio, I needed permission from Jock's widow Flo to tell his story. She knew about

DREAMING OF VIAGRA

'Dreaming of Viagra'. She had been present when I told Jock about it. She had seen Jock's only tear in my presence. She was aware of the impact the poem had on Jock's sense of being supported by me.

Flo was also a patient of mine. I saw her frequently for grief counselling after Jock died. She struggled in coming to terms with Jock's death. She was angry with some aspects of the care he received while in hospital. She was angry with herself for not being there when Jock had his sudden fatal heart attack. And she was angry that he had to suffer so much in the last few years of his life.

I sat with Flo as she experienced this anger. Experience told me it would pass. She was having difficulty letting go of her anger. To her, Jock's death seemed so harsh. So shocking.

Flo loved the idea of the 'Dreaming of Viagra' story being shared on national radio. She wanted to know when the program was going to be broadcast. She rearranged her shift as a volunteer at the local op shop so she could listen to the interview. She told her children about it. She told her friends about it.

When I saw Flo after the radio interview, something had shifted. She appeared a little lighter. We spent most of that visit talking about the interview. She was able to express the gratitude she felt for the care I had offered Jock. She told me about how much he valued our conversations. And how, even if I could do little to relieve his pain, coming to see me and talking about football made him feel a little easier.

Most importantly, after hearing Jock's story on the radio, Flo told me that she was now able to find some meaning and purpose in his suffering. That perhaps his story may have helped someone else. That maybe another person somewhere out there in radio-land might feel a little less alone in their suffering having heard Jock's story.

Flo thanked me for honouring Jock's story in the way I had done. She continued to thank me for doing this as I cared for her during her terminal journey with leukaemia over the next two years.

I think Flo would also be happy to know that this story is being shared with you right now.

TALKING TO A DEAD MAN

Why, oh why, do people like you always come in at the end of the day? Don't you know that your appointment is for just fifteen minutes? How am I supposed to deal with all your complicated issues in such a short time? Didn't the hospital give you some paperwork? A discharge summary or list of medications? Anything that might help me as your new GP?

I don't understand how you can be on so many drugs and know so little about them. And your son, he's no help. He's supposed to be your carer, but he knows even less than you. Not surprising really. He's an academic. No wonder he has no practical good sense.

This is going to take a lot of visits to get sorted. I guess we're going to get to know each other much better during this time.

Can you please stop asking me about your back pain. I've told you it's from your arthritis. There are so many other more important things to sort out – your diabetes, rehab after your stroke, getting your blood pressure down, making sure you take the right puffers for your emphysema. And heaven forbid that I could ever make you stop smoking and drinking. So can we deal with your back pain another time please?

Even after all these visits, when I try to sort out your medical problems, I've still got questions I haven't found the time to ask you. How did you survive to be nearly ninety with so many medical problems? Did you get hooked on the smokes when you were an

eighteen-year-old Rat of Tobruk? Was your buggered liver an occupational hazard from being a travelling alcohol salesman in rural Australia?

Why, oh why, didn't I listen more carefully to your back pain? When will I ever learn? *If I'm feeling rushed, slow down and listen.* At least there are good treatments for metastatic prostate cancer. The radiotherapy should get rid of your pain. And the hormones will slow its progress.

Why couldn't the cancer unit just do what they were asked – give you a short course of radiotherapy? Why did they have to fiddle with your pain medications? We had things just right before you went in.

The story your son told me about his visit to you while you were in hospital made me laugh. 'I went to see Dad after he'd had the radiotherapy. He was curled up asleep when I got there. It looked like he was bombed out on all the meds they were pumping into him. There was a nurse in the room. She told me how much she enjoyed talking with someone like Dad who'd had such an interesting life. I waited a few minutes to see if he would wake up while the nurse prattled on about I don't know what. It didn't look like he was going to stir. As I leant over to say goodbye, he opened one eye and said, "Psst. Don't go, mate. I'm bunging it on that I'm asleep. I just want that bloody nurse to go away. She won't shut up." Typical Dad!'

Thanks for telling me about how you felt when you were eventually discharged from hospital. Hearing your version of events made my day. 'Getting all those bloody tubes out of me was the best day of my life.' I guess you learnt your stoicism in the army. Using humour to cope with so much suffering.

Your daughter-in-law is an angel the way she cares for you. How she welcomed you into their home. It can't be easy for them. Your grandson had to move onto the veranda so you could have his room. Your wheelchair and commode clog up the narrow hallway. The odour from your smoking (and goodness knows what else) permeates every room. Her loving care must be a healing balm.

Did I ever tell you that I do your home visits on the way to

dropping the kids at school? They sit in the car playing Super Mario Kart on their Nintendos while we talk about your pain, your gratitude for the care your family is giving you, and your ongoing pleasure in being wheeled outside to have a smoke in the sunshine. When I get back in the car, my kids always ask, 'How's Cyril today?'

I love how our conversations are all bookended by a gravely twenty-B&H-a-day, 'G'day Doc, how's things.' And, 'Thanks for coming, Doc. Have a good one.'

Thanks for being so open in our discussions about your wishes for end-of-life care. I wasn't surprised when you said, 'If there's no hope, Doc, put me out of my misery.'

You probably don't remember this, but you've had a near miss. Your cough got worse. You developed a fever. Were barely responsive. And when you were awake, you had no idea of where you were or what was going on. I suggested to your son that it might be wise to call in the rest of the family. Sooner rather than later. When I visited the next day, you surprised me, propped up in bed, holding court with your extended family.

Thank you for generously allowing me to take your photo to use in my teaching of doctors training to become GPs. 'Go your hardest, Doc.' The young doctors rarely do home visits these days. I use your photo to show them how much can be learnt from visiting a person in their own environment. I love telling your story to my students after we've looked at the photo of you perched on the side of your bed below a poster of Jim Morrison, your feet barely reaching the ash-stained carpet. After I've relieved them of the assumptions they've made about you on the basis of their first impressions. Assumptions that I recognise only too well from my first impressions of you.

You've proven my prognostic skills to be lacking on at least three more occasions. Cough. Fever. Confusion. Knocking on heaven's door. Family called in. Reawakening. Your son asked me, 'Hilton, do you ever get anything right?' I think he was only half joking.

Yesterday it looked like you were not going to wake up. Was I finally going to get something right? Your son phones me at home

at 9 pm to check on whether they could give you more morphine to settle your cough and agitation. We make a plan to help keep you comfortable overnight. 'Call me if you have any other questions,' I offer. 'I'll pop by in the morning.'

My wife took our kids to school today. I think this visit might take longer than usual. Your daughter-in-law meets me at the front door in her dressing gown, her hair wet. 'I checked on Cyril before I went for my shower and he was sleeping quietly. I went in again a minute ago. I don't think he's breathing.'

She leads me to your room. I enter for the final time to confirm what we both suspect. Tips of my fingers gently circle your still warm wrist. 'I'm going to feel for your pulse now, Cyril,' I whisper, worried that I might appear mad talking to a dead man. Stethoscope placed over your now silent heart. 'Just listening to your heart, mate.'

I offer my condolences to your family and explain what will happen next. 'I'll do the death and cremation certificates when I get back to the clinic. The funeral director can pick them up from there. Are you okay to call them, or would you like me to do it?'

I'm ashamed to say that I feel a sense of relief now that you've died. Caring for you over the last six years has been a privilege. But also a burden, especially the final weeks. Emotionally draining. The time pressures. So many problems to solve. I'm glad I was able to support you to have the death you wanted, but I do feel guilty about being relieved now that it's all over.

At the dinner table tonight, I tell my kids that you died. We light a candle in your honour. My daughter sheds a tear, even though she never met you.

I'M LOSING MY PATIENTS

The blank death certificate sits in front of me. No matter where a life starts, where it ventures, the Medical Certificate of Cause of Death is the concluding punctuation mark on a person's medical narrative.

I approach the completion of the death certificate with reverence. My final task in the care of a patient. A moment to pause. Reflect. Say goodbye. To honour their life within the rigid confines of a bureaucratic document.

This ritual is becoming increasingly frequent.

My patients have been growing older with me. Despite medicine's advances and my best efforts, they are dying. It is their time. I'm losing my patients.

Just last month, I lost three. Lilly, my oldest patient, was an elegant matriarch. Each of her frequent visits ended with her gently touching my arm and saying, 'Bless you, Hilton.' I had cared for her husband Don before his death. Now it was Lilly's turn. Her heart was failing. 'I hope that one night I will go to sleep and wake up dead. Just like Don did.' Her wish came true a few days ago. *Who is going to bless me now?*

Len had been a child throughout Germany's bombing of London. I had once ruined his Christmas by sending him to hospital to have a heart pacemaker inserted. He would have died without it. He wasn't ready for that. The pacemaker kept him going for another decade. Not always easy years. But, 'Better than the alternative,' as he often said. Len was a poet. Each visit to me was accompanied by the gift of

I'M LOSING MY PATIENTS

a poem, 'From when the muse was upon me.' The last time I saw him he told me he was feeling better than he had for years. Another gift. He woke up dead the following week.

Joe had been a postman during times when delivering the mail included many a garden path conversation. Even as his dementia progressed, Joe still enjoyed animated conversations. I loved how his disconnection with the present transported us to a simpler time. Until that gift too was snuffed out by dementia's relentless march.

I finish writing the death certificate. I pause and offer gratitude for the blessings, the poems, the conversations and all the other gifts my patients have shared with me, and I walk out to greet my next patient. The waiting room is full. Many familiar faces look my way.

I am troubled by a nagging thought. A persistent pestering question.

Who will be next?

FINAL CONVERSATIONS

It was one of those conversations that I wished I had been able to record. It would have made a great example of how to maintain a person's dignity in the face of advanced dementia.

Rose was being admitted to a residential aged-care facility (RACF). I was her GP. We were having a conversation with Rose's two daughters and the RACF staff about the goals of care for Rose's admission.

We got round to the question of what to do if Rose had a serious illness from which there was little chance of recovery, or if the only treatment available required hospital admission. Rose stopped us all in our tracks with her interjection. 'I can see no point in any of that. When your time is up, your time is up. I've had a good life. What's the point in prolonging it?' Rose was very clear. She didn't know what day it was. She didn't know where she was. She would not be able to recall a random name and address or any other elements of the standard Mini-Mental Assessment we use to help assess a person's cognitive functioning. But she was still able to express with absolute clarity her long-held views about end-of-life care. She had expressed these thoughts to me on many previous occasions.

I was reminded of the conversation I'd had with my father when his dementia had progressed to the point where he'd needed full-time care in a nursing home. 'Well, it could be worse. At least I'm not dying,' was his response to being told he would need to move from his

FINAL CONVERSATIONS

home into a RACF. Like Rose, he might not have known what day it was. He might not have known where he was. He would not have been able to recall a random name and address. But he was still able to express with absolute clarity his view that life was still worth living because of the love he received from his long-term partner.

I had known Rose and her husband Carl for over a decade. They had moved to our region to be closer to their daughters. Rose and Carl spent their early married life in inner Sydney, living in a community of artists, actors, American servicemen on R'n'R, drinkers, prostitutes. They lived a colourful life in that milieu. They moved to suburbia when their children came along but retained their sense of mischief. It was a delight to get to know them. I was already caring for their daughter's family, so when they arrived, it was a precious opportunity to be a real family doctor.

Early on in our time together, it became clear that Rose was developing dementia. Her cognitive and functional decline was made worse by her significant visual impairment.

Carl was extremely protective of Rose. As her dementia progressed, and she relied more on Carl for support, he grew even more protective. 'We don't need any interfering do-gooders coming into our home.'

Much of the extra care required fell to their daughters. They both had jobs and school-age children to manage. Try as I might, I could not convince Carl to accept community services. His views were in line with many working-class folk of his generation. 'I made a vow to care for Rose. 'Til death do us part! I'm not letting anyone lock her up.'

We came to an uneasy truce in this battle. Carl agreed that their daughter Jo could join them in their visits with me. Rose was delighted with this arrangement, because each doctor's visit was followed by coffee and cake at her favourite café. And we agreed that they would come regularly, rather than waiting for something to go wrong first. I saw them monthly for many years. And more often at times of need. Together, we managed this dance through heart failure, bowel cancer and repeated urinary tract infections. Despite her increasing ailments

and progressive dementia, Rose always appeared happy, engaged in family activities and well cared for.

Until Carl died suddenly at home. Certifying Carl's death was my first visit to their home. It was a shocking experience. The medications that I had been assiduously prescribing for Rose were jumbled in an old shoebox on the kitchen counter. No wonder some of the drugs didn't seem to be working as I had expected! Who knows if they were even being taken?

I wished that I'd done a home visit earlier. Might this have avoided some of their problems?

I was reminded of a visit to my father's home a few months before his admission to RACF. He had started having falls and they were becoming more frequent. I wondered if removing some items of furniture and the floor rugs in their home might reduce his falls risk, but I didn't want to offend my father and his partner by appearing to be an interfering do-gooder. In retrospect, I wish I'd been more assertive. Might this have avoided some of their problems?

It was only after Carl's death that the impact of Rose's decline on her ability to function independently became obvious. Carl had been covering for her to such an extent that none of us were aware of how impaired Rose had become. Rose clearly needed full-time care. Urgent respite was arranged and she was soon admitted to our local RACF. And that remarkable end-of-life care conversation.

Once in institutional care, and without Carl by her side, Rose's condition declined rapidly. I visited her just before she died. She looked shrunken, her bed too big for her body. She was staring at the ceiling when I arrived.

'Hi Rose, it's Hilton,' I said, as I sat by her side and gently rested my palm on the back of her gnarly hand. She looked up at me and, for a moment, recognition sparked in her eyes before her gaze returned to whatever was occupying her attention before I walked in.

I was reminded of my final visit to see my father before he too died from dementia while in full-time care. Shrunken, his bed too big for his body, he was staring at the ceiling when I arrived.

FINAL CONVERSATIONS

'Hi Dad, it's Hilton,' I said as I sat by his side and gently rested my palm on the back of his gnarly hand. My dad looked up at me and for a moment, there was a sparkle of recognition in his eyes. 'I used to know someone who looked just like you,' he said, before his gaze returned to whatever was occupying his attention before I walked in.

MYSTERY

Questioning Mystery

> The first time I heard the word Mystery I did not understand what it meant. As an avid reader of mystery stories, I had the idea that something is a mystery only because its solution has not yet been found. But mystery is different from Mystery. By its very nature Mystery cannot be solved, can never be known. It can only be lived.
>
> Rachel Remen, *My Grandfather's Blessings*

Why had it been so hard for me to get started on this essay? It's been with me for so long – weeks, months, years. I knew what I wanted to write. I just could not get started.

I wanted to write about a patients who had made an unexpected recovery from advanced melanoma. But it was more than just the telling of his story. I wanted to discover the whys and the hows of his recovery. Why him? How did he do it? I wanted to discover what role I may have played and to learn how doctors might assist in such a recovery.

So I did the research. I spoke at length with my patient about his views of what had transpired. I reviewed the medical literature. 'Spontaneous remission' and 'spontaneous regression' are the terms used. As if it happens by magic. These articles lead to other articles on the placebo effect. Articles with promises of cures for cancer from

MYSTERY

multiple non-medical modalities. Articles by self-proclaimed medical sceptics who don't believe in such recoveries.

But still I couldn't get started on this essay. I couldn't find the thread that would bind my thoughts together. What was my angle? What was I really trying to say? I had the facts of the story, but the understanding of the meaning of the facts eluded me.

Stream of consciousness – or free – writing can be a way to free up thinking. I teach it in the reflective writing workshops I run for doctors and other health professionals. This simple process can have profound affects. It involves using a current problem as the starting point for twenty minutes of writing. I invite people to start with an enquiring mind. With the words *I wonder* … and then start writing. Keeping the pen moving. Let the pen guide the writing. No stopping. No worrying about spelling or grammar or neatness. Leaving your inner critic aside.

I reached for my pencil and pad and began.

I wonder why I can't get started on writing this essay. Maybe it's because … and I was away. Within a few moments of starting, it became clear to me that the theme for my essay was uncertain – despite having all the facts for the story – because *uncertainty in the face of the facts* was the very theme of the story! I was grasping for something that could not be grasped. I was trying to use my logical, rational, scientific mind to grasp something mercurial. I could see its shimmering surface reflecting my ideas, but it kept slipping through my fingers.

Trying to understand healing is like that for me. I can see that it happens. I know it is real. But I can't actually see it. Or touch it. I don't know where it lives. I'm not sure where it does its work. It eludes my senses. And so, it is hard for me to make sense of it.

There are other doctors, many other doctors, who may not have tried to understand healing. They may not have chosen to wrestle with this dilemma, opened Pandora's Box. They live in a world of randomised double-blind controlled trials, the gold standard for medical research. They live in a reductionist world of guidelines and flow charts and

computer-assisted diagnostic aids. They live in a world of certainty. They live with the illusion, or perhaps delusion, that we can understand everything. They have both feet firmly planted on the rational, scientific, medicine side of the fence. How I envy them at times.

Of course, this scientific approach to medicine has brought forward our understanding of disease and diagnosis and treatment. Of course, this scientific approach saves lives every day. I value this scientific approach in the work I do.

But it doesn't tell me everything. It doesn't help me to understand where healing takes place. Or why it happens for some people and not for others. We have not been raised to cultivate a sense of Mystery.

On the opposite side of this seemingly impenetrable fence sit the shamans. Masters of ancient healing wisdom. Gentle people. Layers on of hands. Acceptors of mystery. They are not bound by the rigours of the scientific method. They live in a world of spirit and energy. Meridians and chakras.

I don't always share their faith that what they are doing is really helping people. I don't always understand their rationale. Or their methods. But how I envy their approach at times. What would it take for me to be more like them?

I find myself in the uncomfortable position of having one foot on either side of this fence. One foot on the side of rational, scientific medicine. The other foot on the side of energy, healing and mystery. Standing with one foot on one side of a picket fence, with the other foot on the other side of the fence, can only have one result. A picket poking right where it hurts most! I needed to shift something. Maybe writing this piece could help to deepen my understanding. To offer enlightenment. To remove some of the pressure from that damned picket! Or even better, to break down the fence entirely.

And so, I write ...

Savouring Mystery
The first time I laid eyes on Jason, the waiting room was full. I was running late. I came out to get my next patient, seeing many familiar

MYSTERY

faces. Some were chatting with their neighbours, as happens in the waiting room of a country town family practice. Some were reading the out-of-date magazines on offer. And there, sitting under the window, was a man on the edge of his seat. A stranger to me. Ten or fifteen pairs of eyes looked up as I entered the waiting room. 'Is it finally my turn?' the eyes ask. But his eyes were different. Seeking. Searching. 'Is this one the doctor I will be seeing? Does he match the description I was given of him by my last doctor?'

I didn't know that about him yet. But I did know that his creased facial expression and angular Tin Man posture told me he was anxious. And his complexion told me that he was sick.

It is hard to grasp the words to describe what it was about his complexion that told me he was sick. Pallor is the medical word, but he wasn't really pale. Maybe sallow is a better description. 'Of the skin or complexion, a sickly yellow or pale brown', says the *Oxford Concise Australian Dictionary*, and that nearly gets it.

We were taught at medical school to remember pathognomonic features – physical signs which always meant a certain diagnosis. We were told they are like elephants; once seen, never forgotten. Jason had the pathognomonic signs of an anxious, sick man. I have not forgotten it, but I find it difficult to adequately describe it.

Jason had good reason for looking sick. He had recently had neurosurgery to remove three melanoma deposits from his brain. He had just completed a course of radiotherapy. At the time of our first meeting, he had two new melanomas growing in his brain, but we didn't know that yet. He had a melanoma growing in his lung, but we didn't know that yet. He had a melanoma growing on his adrenal gland, but we didn't know that yet either. He was thirty-seven years old.

Jason had good reason for looking anxious. In the preceding twelve months, he had seen many doctors. Most of them had told him that he was going to die. The surgeon who removed the advanced melanoma from his arm told him he had a ten per cent chance of living more than five years. The head of the cancer unit, who he saw when he had melanomas growing in his brain, told him he had two weeks to live.

To not bother having any treatment because nothing would work. To go home and die. Jason sought other advice. He found a GP to assist him in the process. He saw a neurosurgeon who was willing to operate on his brain tumours. He found a radiotherapist willing to give him radiotherapy.

And now, he was coming to see a new doctor. He was coming to see me. His previous GP was a former student of mine who had suggested that I would be a good person to care for Jason when he moved from the city to my area. Over the next two years, I endeavoured to support Jason as he had surgery for the multiple melanoma tumours in his brain, his left lung, and his right adrenal gland.

If the research predicted that Jason had a ten per cent chance of surviving five years with an advanced aggressive melanoma on his arm, I can't even imagine how gloomy the outlook would be for someone with five brain tumours, a large lung tumour, and one invading a whole adrenal gland. No double-blind controlled trials would have been done on this population of patients. Jason may be the only person ever with this unique constellation of disease. How could rational scientific medicine be relied upon in these circumstances?

But Jason always remained hopeful. And so did I. He told me that he did not believe in the 'Morbid recitation of medical statistics', which was the preferred method of conveying Jason's future to him by the oncologists and melanoma specialists he had seen. He also refused to believe that he was a 'Fated object moving along a conveyor belt to an inevitable destiny'. Jason had a PhD in the study of paradigms. He found this training crucial in enabling him to maintain his optimism despite the morbid statistics. He understood that the medical model could be helpful, but that it was not the only way to look at reality. 'Statistics give a historical snapshot, but they may not be true for me.'

Jason's philosophical beliefs helped him. 'The future is an open possibility. Because some things are more likely, it doesn't mean that they are inevitable.' Jason made the decision to choose a trajectory for himself that did not involve dying in the immediate future. He became highly aware of his mortality, and this helped him to savour

MYSTERY

the joyous moments in his life and to focus on hope rather than despair.

Jason spoke in glowing terms about his current neurosurgeon. 'We used to have conversations about the uncertainty of my situation. While he clearly preferred to have a sense of control, he did still seem comfortable to sit with the uncertainty in my case. I bought him a book on the nature of hope. He bought me a Superman T-shirt.'

It was not easy for me to always focus on hope rather than despair for Jason's situation. I didn't have his training in paradigms. My medical training was telling me to think the worst, while my heart was telling me to hope for the best. Thinking the worst. Hoping for the best. At times, this was exhausting. But I never gave up on what I described as My Jason Project. To help him live life as full as possible and to prove all those gloomy predictions wrong.

A few weeks before Jason was booked to have surgery to remove his adrenal gland, there was a dreadful moment. The new lesions on his liver scans were interpreted as being cancer deposits (they ended up being benign non-cancerous cysts when biopsied during the surgery, but when someone is known to have metastatic melanoma, and they have lesions on their liver scans, it is hard for the radiologist not to report them as melanomas). Jason was reluctantly considering whether to have major surgery to try to remove his adrenal gland and these tumours from his liver.

The day for his surgery approached. Jason came to ask me what I thought he should do. Should he go ahead with this massive surgery? Or should he try other approaches? As we were talking about his options, I had what I can only describe as a vision. A most disturbing disorientating vision.

I saw Jason dead.

Dead on the operating table. Dead from the surgery.

I didn't imagine it. I saw it. It was real. It completely filled my mind's eye. I began a silent inner panic.

What am I supposed to do with this? Nothing like this has ever happened before.

ONE CURIOUS DOCTOR

Occasionally, I have thoughts or ideas which seem to spring from nowhere. There may be moments when I get a sense of something. Of one possible future outcome or a preferred path to suggest. But this wasn't a sense. An essence. It was real. Tangible. I was seeing Jason's death. Playing out in my mind. While he was sitting in front of me.

My medical training in no way prepared me for dealing with such a premonition. Does shaman school offer guidance for these moments?

The best I could do was to suggest that we end our conversation for the moment and arrange to meet again in a week. He still had some time to make his final decision. This suggestion was ostensibly to give Jason an opportunity to think about what we had discussed. In reality, it was to give me a chance to deal with the panic churning inside of me.

What should I do when I see Jason next? Should I tell him about this vision? Was it fair to put my (possibly completely irrational) fear onto him? But what if the vision turns out to be an accurate premonition and I don't say anything? How will I be able to live with myself after that?

This was uncharted territory for me. There was no medical research to help me navigate an evidence-based path. And it was definitely too weird to casually discuss with colleagues in the tearoom.

I chose not to tell Jason about my vision. He had enough to worry about without me burdening him with my worries. I nearly cried at his final visit before the surgery. I thought it might be the last time I saw him.

But I did see him again. He survived his surgery. And continues to be well, defying all the medical odds. Once Jason had fully recovered, I did discuss my vision with him. He was generous in his response. He said that I had seen one possible outcome, but that it didn't have to be the inevitable truth. His interpretation of why I had the vision when I did was because he was at that time booked with a different surgeon to the one who finally did the operation. 'After the operation, they told me that the surgery ended up being much more complex than anticipated and how lucky I was to have had that particular

MYSTERY

surgeon operating on me. Maybe if the original surgeon had done the operation, your vision would have come true.'

There is so much that goes on between a doctor and a patient that can never be understood. This experience with Jason adds to the long list of mysteries in my medical life. His training in paradigms was more helpful than my medical training at explaining what might have been going on. I value these mysteries. They help me to feel alive. Engaged. Curious. I was never quite sure why I seemed to relish these surprises until I read the work of American physician Rachel Remen. In her book, *My Grandfather's Blessings*, she talks about such moments.

> Perhaps real wisdom lies in not seeking answers at all. Any answer we find will not be true for long. An answer is a place where we can fall asleep as life moves past us to its next question. After all these years I have begun to wonder if the secret of living well is not in having all the answers but in pursuing unanswerable questions in good company.

Jason and I continue to ponder unanswerable questions in each other's company. It remains a privilege to be part of his team.

DIARY OF A ~~WIMPY~~ WOUNDED DOC

Sunday 20 January

Tomorrow is my first day back at work after our annual summer pilgrimage to the Brooms Head beach shack.

I wonder how I'll go.

Monday 21 January

At dawn, I commence my workday burnout prevention ritual. Stretching. Aerobic exercise. Resistance exercise. Qui gong. Mindfulness meditation. Reflective writing.

Will these practices help me hang onto the holiday glow?

My first patient for the day is Jackson, a five-year-old boy coming back for review after starting simple treatments for dust mite allergy a month ago. 'We've got our son back, thanks to you,' beams his mum. 'I can't believe what a difference the spray made. Jax is sleeping all night, he's stopped snoring and his bed doesn't look like a disaster zone when he wakes up. He's so much happier. It's like a miracle. You've become our family superhero, Hilton!'

So far, so good. The glow remains intact.

By 5.45 pm, I am seeing my twenty-eighth patient for the day. There are two more people in the waiting room. *How could the post-holiday glow vanish so quickly?* This patient has had months of chronic, unrelenting neck-pain. *I have too.* She wakes up in pain dozens of times each night. *I do too.* All the treatments she has tried have

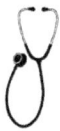

failed. *Mine have too.* She is at a loss about what to do next. *I am too.*

I struggle to maintain my focus on the patient's story.

How am I going to learn to live with this?

Monday 28 January

It only took a week and already I've had to curtail my morning burnout prevention ritual to do a home visit before starting work at the medical centre.

Why do I always try to squeeze these visits in before or after work? During my personal time? Why is it so hard for me to schedule them during normal working hours?

Wednesday 30 January

My colleague Pete and I are sharing our regular lunchtime debrief on a park bench overlooking Seven Mile Beach. We sit side by side, looking over the rocky reef to the cloud mountains on the horizon. Like doing a road trip with adolescent children, it's easier to have a meaningful conversation without the intensity of eye contact. It's my turn for a whinge.

'I don't know what I was thinking when I decided to do an extra afternoon's work at the clinic. I hoped it might ease the waiting time for people to get in to see me. That lasted about a week! Now the backlog is just as bad as ever and I'm not getting an afternoon off! What a stupid idea that was!'

Pete sits back, nods in that familiar 'I told you so, mate' way, which I do my best to ignore.

'Bloody hell, is that the time already? Wish we could sit here all arvo. But I suppose we'd better start heading back.'

Thursday 31 January

It's weird how things seem to come in runs. Today it's all mental health. Until, in the middle of seeing one of my long-term depressed patients, the phone rings. I interrupt the patient and take the call. The receptionist tells me that the police want to speak with me.

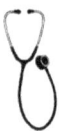

Just when the day couldn't get any worse.

'It's Constable Pierce here, Doctor. Your patient Carl Lucas has been found dead in his home. We need you to come down and identify the body as soon as you can.'

I turn back to the patient. 'There's an emergency I've got to attend to. Sorry about this. Can't be helped. Tell the receptionists to squeeze you in this afternoon or tomorrow.'

I ask our practice manager to reschedule the rest of the morning's patients, and I grab my bag. To avoid a sea of needy gazes from the expectant faces in the full waiting room, I exit through the back door.

This is going to be a nightmare. I always thought Rose would be the first to go. How the hell am I going to manage things for her now?

Carl is (or was, I should now say) a loveable rogue. I'd cared for him and his wife Rose, who has dementia and partial blindness, for over fifteen years. I guided their daughter Jo through IVF. I have known Carl's two grand-daughters since they were each a + sign on Jo's pregnancy test strips.

As I step from the sanctity of my car, my mind focuses on the task ahead.

Here we go again. Entering another house of grief.

Jo meets me at the front door.

How is it that fresh grief always has such a pungent odour?

'I'm sorry for your loss, Jo.'

'Thanks Hilton, and thanks for coming around so quickly. We think Dad died a couple of days ago. Mum's dementia is so bad that she didn't realise what had happened. She thought he was having a long session at the pub. Dad's half hidden on the floor beside his bed. Mum couldn't see him lying there.'

I enter the house. The police officer's silent greeting says, *Well, this sucks, doesn't it! Why do we do this bloody job?*

I find Carl face down on the floor in his usual attire – faded tracksuit pants and oversized flannelette shirt. His skin is a maze of mottled purple with blotches of indigo blue.

DIARY OF A ~~WIMPY~~ WOUNDED DOC

I don't think I've ever seen anyone look so very, very dead. I'm definitely not going to need to listen for heart sounds to certify poor old Carl!

Back at the medical centre, I complete Carl's death certificate. I flick back through the pad, reading the long list of patients I have lost, all recorded in my stilted attempt at neat handwriting. I close the pad and lock it in the bottom drawer of my desk. 'Bye Carl, I'll miss you,' I say to my empty room.

I hope Pete is ready for lunch.

Saturday 2 February

We take possession of a new VW Transporter Frontline campervan. With my wife's encouragement, we're buying it a couple of years earlier than planned. 'We shouldn't wait until you retire. Who knows what might happen? Let's do it now.'

As we drive home from the dealer, I'm struck by the immediate anticipatory joy that has come from buying the van.

Saturday 9 February

I head off for my first solo trip in the campervan to Bundjalung National Park. I pull up at the campsite. Climb into the back of the van. Unclip four straps. Lift the pop-top. And I am set up.

I'm set!

Sunday 10 February

At dawn, I wander down the track to Back Beach, alone apart from scatterings of kangaroos. Brahminy kites circle overhead. I pause to photograph the sun coming up behind rock platforms. When I reach the end of the beach, I take off my clothes and swim naked. I sit on the rocks to dry off. The early morning sun warms my body. I feel enlivened in a way that, until this moment, was a distant memory. I begin to weep as my mind becomes an ocean of questions.

When was the last time I noticed the world's tiny details? How long has it been since I last had a skinny dip?

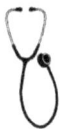

How many other important things have I been neglecting? How could I forget what it feels like to be alive?

How could I let this happen? What have they done to me?

Monday 11 February

At dawn, I commence my workday burnout prevention ritual. Stretching. Aerobic exercise. Resistance exercise. Qui gong. Mindfulness meditation. Reflective writing.

Will these practices help me hang onto the holiday glow?

As I'm finishing breakfast, I begin weeping again. 'I was feeling so alive this time yesterday. I don't want to go back to work. It's killing me.'

My wife responds with a hug. I steel myself for work.

I'm running twenty minutes late by the time I'm with my third patient for the morning. Like all my patients, she is elderly with complex insoluble problems. Her husband died two weeks ago. She is not coping well on her own. She is in constant pain from arthritis. Her diabetes is out of control but she doesn't care about that. All she wants to do is drive 800 kilometres to see her daughter. For the last ten years, she hasn't driven further than the shops because her husband used to do all the driving.

As I listen to my patient, I notice that I'm distractedly rubbing my right cheek.

A new fear gains traction and a silent crescendo voice. *What's this damned numbness? I've never had this before. This could be bad. Real bad.*

After seeing off the widow, I tell Pete about the numbness. He responds with what I already know. 'You need to go to Emergency. You need to get scans to make sure you're not having a stroke.'

My wife picks me up and takes me to the hospital. Examinations show no signs of stroke. I am booked for an MRI scan the next morning.

As we're driving home, my wife asks how I am feeling. 'I can hardly feel the numbness now. Maybe it was all in my head. That's what the Emergency doctor implied. It's embarrassing, but better than a stroke.'

DIARY OF A ~~WIMPY~~ WOUNDED DOC

Tuesday 12 February

As I enter the MRI scanner, the radiographer tells me that the examination will take about forty minutes. The bed is narrow and hard. My head is clamped in a brace, my arms strapped by my side. The scanner belts around my head. Once again, my mind is filled with unexpected thoughts.

This is the most peaceful I have felt on a workday morning for ages. No one can get to me here. My eyes jolt open.

If this feels peaceful, tethered to a slab less comfortable than our kitchen table, with a scanner jackhammering in my face, then I'm in big trouble!

Wednesday 13 February

I have an appointment with my doctor. After telling me the scans are normal, he asks how I am doing. The floodgates open.

'Work is terrible. My patients are all so hard to manage. They are a litany of co-morbidities. Guidelines don't apply to them. Three died on me last month. I agonise about who will be next. I write long lists of things I need to do to keep on top of their care. They've infected my dreams. I dread going to work. I never used to be like this. I've tried everything to get back on track but nothing is working. I'm terrified that I'm going to kill someone. I haven't killed anyone in thirty-eight years of doctoring. I don't want to start now! I'd never forgive myself if that happened. I'd hate to end my career like that.'

My doctor sits back and says with calm clarity, 'You're done.'

'Done? What do you mean, done?'

'You can't go back to work. It's no good for you.'

I take this in, the news that my body has been trying to give me for months.

'We're one doctor short for a couple of weeks. I don't want to let the team down. How about I work until next Friday and then take some time off?' *What would they think of me if I didn't show up to work while we are short staffed?*

'No, you're done. You need to make that call.'

Helping my daughter with her English homework that evening is a distraction from my distress. We are reading T.S. Eliot's 'The Hollow Men'. The final line feels like it's been written about me: 'This is how the world ends, not with a bang but a whimper.' *Am I a hollow, whimpering man?*

Thursday 14 February

After lying awake most of the night rehearsing what to say, I make the dreaded call to our practice manager.

'I can't come into work. My doctor has advised extended leave. I don't know when I'll be able to return. Sorry to be such a nuisance.'

I struggle to fight back tears, feeling like the embodiment of a Hollow Man. She thanks me for calling and wishes me well. *Was her brevity out of respect for my distress or a reflection of her annoyance?*

My reward after such a difficult conversation is sharing a coffee with my wife on our back veranda. We haven't done this together on a Thursday morning for years. It's the perfect Valentine's Day gift.

'I can't believe how much better I feel. The guilt, it seems to be evaporating. I still feel ashamed and embarrassed, but the guilt, it's feeling better already. I should have listened to you and done this months ago.'

Monday 18 February

My other job involves writing clinical guidelines for family doctors. I am working on the PTSD guideline. I read the diagnostic criteria.

Holy shit! That is me. I do tick all those boxes. Maybe my doctor was right.

I read the recommended treatments. The guidelines say avoiding triggers is a crucial part of the management of PTSD.

Does this mean I don't have to feel guilty about needing time off work?

I pause, look up and gently touch my right cheek where it was numb exactly one week ago.

Does this mean I haven't just been weak? Maybe this has all been unavoidable.

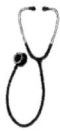

The guidelines also say that some personality types are more prone to PTSD.

Maybe I'm one of those people and it was always going to happen, even with everything I've been doing to try to stay well. Does this mean it's not my fault?

PTSD.

That's not a weakness.

It feels more like a badge of honour. I can learn to live with that!

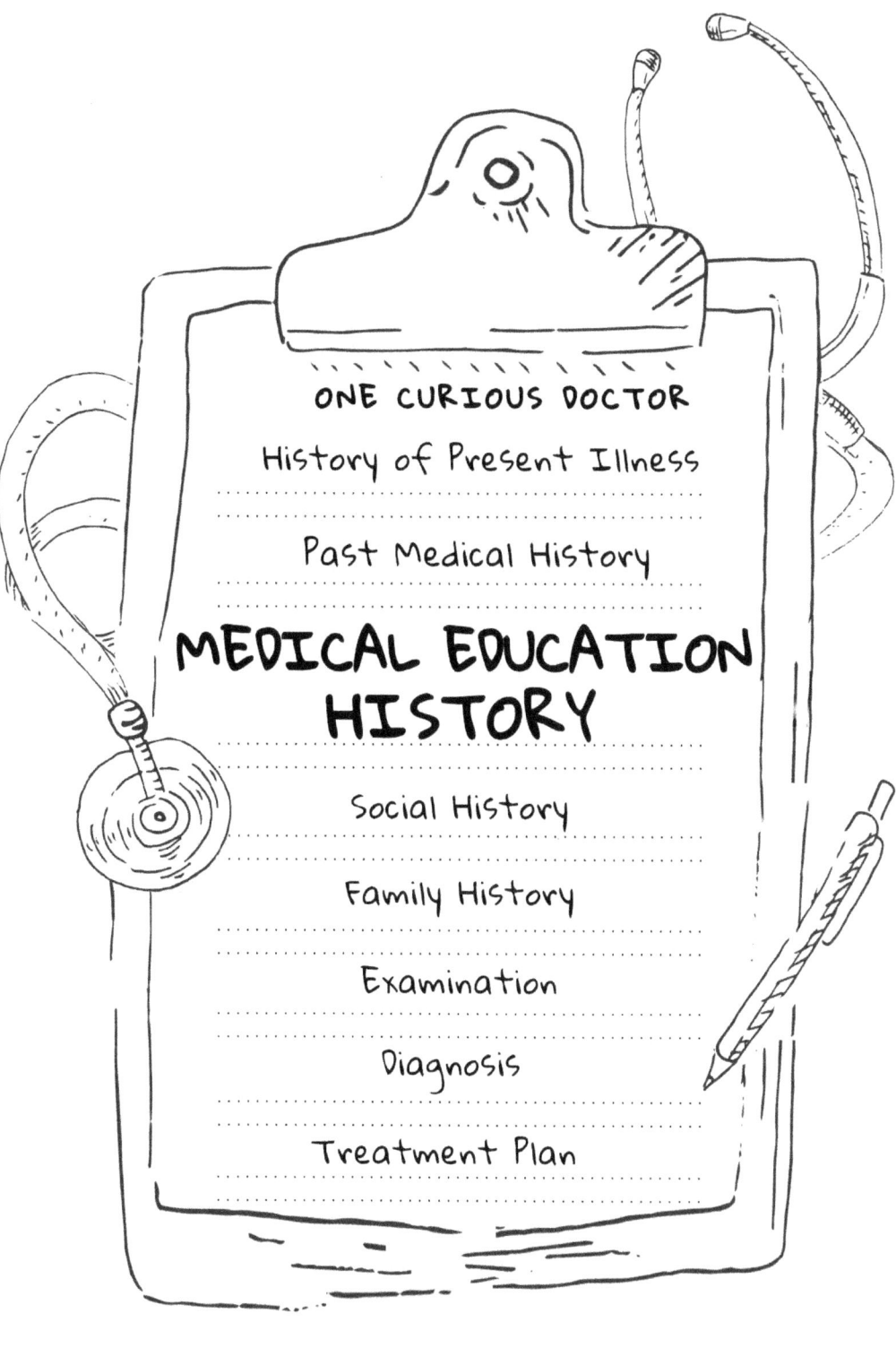

EIGHT SEASONS

SANDRA'S STORY, PART 2

I have continued to care for Sandra and her family despite our rocky start. I met Sandra's parents when her father developed dementia. I would see Sandra's husband and other daughter for routine visits.

We were all delighted that Tahlia remained in remission. She had some ongoing health issues as a consequence of the treatment for leukaemia, but she became a positive, engaging, active young woman. She played netball at the same club as my daughter. They shared the same dance studio. It brought me much joy to see Tahlia outside my work environment. Seeing her so full of life.

Sandra went back to work as a psychologist. We began sharing clients in a professional capacity.

Tahlia's remission has been a challenge for Sandra. It was easy for her fears to bubble to the surface. If Tahlia got sick, as all kids do, Sandra's mind might wander to frightening thoughts. Like when Tahlia once got headaches with a bout of sinusitis. Any mention of headaches triggered memories of Tahlia's cancer diagnosis. Together we have tried to steer a course that acknowledges these fears and takes steps to address them without subjecting Tahlia to unnecessary tests or treatments. It has been a challenging dance. But I think we are doing okay.

One of the most difficult times for Sandra was when Tahlia came off her treatment. On the one hand, Sandra was delighted that Tahlia would no longer need all those medications. But she also knew that

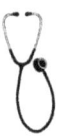

the drugs had put Tahlia into remission. What would happen when the drugs were stopped? How would the leukaemia be controlled now? What if there was one stray leukaemia cell lurking in her bone marrow?

Sandra developed strategies to help transform her fears into meaningful activity. Taking action to make it easier for other parents whose children had leukaemia was one such strategy. What information would have helped her when Tahlia was first diagnosed? How to best navigate the long road through treatment? And how to cope when that treatment eventually stops?

She began writing a pamphlet for parents of children with newly diagnosed leukaemia, aimed at answering these questions. But Sandra is not a person to hold back once she gets started on something. The idea for a pamphlet mushroomed into a book. It detailed Sandra's experiences of the first two years of Tahlia's illness. Sandra asked me if I would proofread *Eight Seasons* before it went to the publisher. I was touched that she sought my input. I devoured the manuscript on a flight to Sydney, weeping quietly into the window beside me at the beauty of her writing and the poignancy of her story.

While *Eight Seasons* had been written primarily for parents of children with leukaemia or other life-threatening illnesses, I thought it would also be perfect for the new doctors I teach. Sandra's writing gives such a clear insight into what it is like to have a child with a serious illness. I am always trying to help my students gain an understanding of what it is like to be in the patient's shoes. *Eight Seasons* did that better than I ever could.

And so began the next dance that Sandra and I needed to negotiate. I was their family doctor. My primary duty of care was to do all that I could to ensure the best possible outcomes for Sandra and Tahlia.

The medical profession has clear guidelines and ethical standards to ensure that doctors make decisions in the best interests of their patients. In medical jargon, it is called having a clear doctor–patient boundary. Don't have an inappropriate relationship (usually meaning

a sexual relationship) with a patient. Don't reveal a patient's personal information to other people. Don't seek personal advantage from being a person's doctor. Failing to maintain a clear doctor–patient boundary can put patient safety at risk and can put the doctor at risk of professional misconduct.

In my line of work, blurred boundaries can be risky business.

I wanted to ask Sandra if we could buy copies of *Eight Seasons* to distribute to my students before their child health workshop. I was aware that by doing so, I was in danger of blurring our patient–doctor boundary. I needed to keep Sandra's best interests in mind. Not mine as a teacher. Nor those of my students.

Sandra had been invited to speak about her book at a Leukaemia Foundation event. She told me how much work she had put into preparing for this presentation.

I began conjuring up an additional plan for our journey. A path that would break new ground. *Why waste all that effort on just one event? Why not ask Sandra to do it again? This time, for my students. After they'd had a chance to read* Eight Seasons.

These ideas were bringing us to the brink of murky territory. All that I knew about Sandra's book and her upcoming speaking engagement had come from her visits to my clinic. Conversations in a sacred space. Would it be okay to break the sanctity of this space, and discuss the possibility of us purchasing copies of her book for my students? Or of her speaking to the students at one of their regular education events?

I wrestled with this dilemma. I knew how passionate Sandra was about trying to make things easier for other parents of children with life-threatening illness. What better way to do that than by speaking directly with the next generation of doctors?

But I was also fearful of doing harm. What if Sandra got stage fright? Or if the students were rude or dismissive? Unlikely outcomes but, like all things in medicine, I needed to balance the risks against the benefit.

I discussed my plans with a trusted colleague. The potential

advantages and the possible risks. He supported the idea. 'If you do it well, it could be an opportunity for Sandra to heal some of the hurt from her experiences over the last few years. And it would be an amazing opportunity for transformative learning for your students. You can't get that sort of stuff from a textbook!'

With those words of encouragement, I made the decision to take the lead in this bold new dance. I took the first steps in the clinic room. Not while we were seated in our assigned positions as patient and doctor. I did it once the medical business of the visit was over. As we stood facing each other, more as equals.

I had rehearsed my offer. 'I've had an idea about an exciting opportunity for your book. Would you be interested in hearing about it?'

Sandra looked surprised. 'Y … yes?' she ventured tentatively as her gaze dropped to the floor.

Ignoring the sinking feeling in my stomach, which I feared might be a mirror of Sandra's emotions, I blurted it out. 'I'd like to buy some copies of *Eight Seasons* and ask the young doctors I teach to read it before their child health workshop.'

Sandra looked up and leant slightly forward. I took a breath and continued. 'And I think it would be amazing if you could also come to the workshop so that the doctors could talk with you about the book and your journey with Tahlia over the last few years.'

Her face became flushed. She fidgeted with her purse. I waited.

'The idea of young doctors reading the book, that sounds amazing. Thank you so much for that. I love the idea that *Eight Seasons* might help some parents.'

I nodded.

'But having to talk to a group of doctors! I don't know if I can do that.'

Sandra's hesitancy told me it was time to draw this part of the conversation to an end. I suggested she give these ideas some thought, and that perhaps we could discuss it at another time. I offered to give her my email address to help keep in touch.

Sandra emailed me a week later and accepted my invitation to

speak with the students. We arranged to meet a few weeks before the education event to discuss how we would manage the session. Choosing a venue for our planning meeting was a challenge. The office of my teaching job seemed the most appropriate. Not the medical clinic. Not either of our homes. Not a local café. So much to think about when entering unchartered territory!

Sandra seemed a little on edge when we met. She brought along a prepared speech. As we went through what she planned to say, she scrawled notes in red pen over her typed manuscript. The further we went, the more I sensed Sandra's growing discomfort. This was the last thing I wanted. As we were speaking, my mind was working overtime. *How can I make this as easy as possible for Sandra?*

Years of practice of listening to people's stories while at the same time trying to come up with a plan to help them enabled me to find a possible solution.

'Instead of you preparing a speech, how about I just ask you some questions? Like an interview. Then you don't have to prepare anything. You are already the expert of your own story. All you will need to do is turn up. I'll take responsibility for the preparation. And for everything else.'

My simple suggestion had an immediate impact on Sandra. She put her pen down. Stopped making notes. Sat back and smiled for the first time during our conversation. 'Can we really do that? That would be fantastic.'

And it was fantastic. Sandra's segment at our child health workshop was brilliant. Sandra and I sat at the front of the room, positioned not too differently to how we would meet in my clinic room. Chairs at a 90-degree angle towards each other, but without the corner of my desk to separate us.

I began the session by asking Sandra some gentle questions. 'How long have you lived in the area?' 'What work do you do?' 'Can you tell us a little about your family?' We then moved on to the details of Tahlia's diagnosis and subsequent treatments. Sandra responded to these prompts with poise and grace.

The time came to open the session to the students. Most of them had read *Eight Seasons*. The students asked Sandra questions with a kindness, compassion and genuine desire to learn more, which warmed the heart of this old doctor. *The future of medicine is in good hands with these fine young doctors.*

Sandra's honesty and courage in response to their questions had a profound impact. What she shared could never be learnt from a textbook or an online module. As my colleague had suggested, it was indeed a transformative experience for all of us present in that room.

There is a saying, which I believe comes from Buddhist philosophy that I try to apply in my teaching.

To sit with the warm breath of the master is the best way to learn.

Sandra is a master. A master of being a parent of a child with leukaemia. If it takes 10,000 hours of practice to gain some level of mastery in a specific field, then by my calculations, Sandra is a master five times over in her journey with Tahlia.

I could never teach the students what Sandra shared. I may have some limited expertise in medical practice and education principles, but Sandra was the real expert during this session. As an educator for over twenty years, watching the way the learners were affected by Sandra and her story was a revelation. Why hadn't I thought to do this sort of thing before?

Sandra is now a regular guest at our annual child health workshops. She is more relaxed with each presentation and has grown in confidence as I support her to share her passionate message.

I am so happy that I took a risk and broke with the conventional medical practice of keeping the patient–doctor relationship contained within the bounds of the clinic room. Inviting Sandra to partner with me in our delicate dance has enhanced rather than harmed the therapeutic aspects of our relationship.

LITERARY MEDICINE

All I knew about Iowa before I went there was that it was home to Radar O'Reilly from the television sitcom *M*A*S*H**. References to Iowa were mostly farcical. An American friend in Australia teased me when I told her I was going to Iowa City. 'Why would you want to go there? It's what we call "fly-over country". No one chooses to go there!'

I chose Iowa City because of its strong literary pedigree. The University of Iowa can claim Pulitzer Prize-winning authors Tennessee Williams and Philip Roth. Tom Irving and Ann Patchett are alumni of the Iowa Writers' Workshop. A UNESCO award recognised this literary history in 2008 when it declared Iowa City its third City of Literature. The first two were Edinburgh and Melbourne.

My visit to Iowa was going to be my first opportunity to present a writing workshop in the USA, a first foray into American medical humanities. My workshops had been quite successful in the small Australian medical humanities pond. I'm not sure what possessed me to think that I might be able to swim with the big fish in America. I was about to find out.

The University of Iowa's medical school embraces Iowa's literary tradition. It integrates the arts into medical education, with a particular emphasis on writing. Each year, they host The Examined Life Conference, referencing Socrates' claim that an 'Unexamined life is not worth living'. The conference explores links between the science of medicine and the art of writing. I was delighted when the

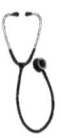

Examined Life team accepted my proposal to present my writing workshop at their 2011 conference.

My teaching at the conference was well received. Perhaps it was because my presentations were raw and uncluttered by academic dogma. Just a few simple ideas cutting to the core of what it means to work as a doctor.

This positive response bolstered my ego and gave me confidence. So much confidence that I asked Dave, the conference organiser, if I could read one of my stories at the open mic reading session on the second night of the conference. I hadn't put my name down for the reading night because I didn't believe I could make a worthwhile contribution. While I felt moderately confident as a facilitator of writing workshops, I did not feel credentialed as a writer. Dave agreed to add my name to the list of readers.

The reading night was to be held at the Prairie Lights Bookstore, Iowa City's independent bookshop. Its fame extends beyond being a repository for books written by Iowa's literary luminaries. It is traditional for American presidential candidates to deliver an address at the bookshop during their electoral campaign. Barack Obama had spoken there during his march to the White House. The walls of the bookshop were covered. There were photos of Obama's visit, speaking from the small podium in the reading room, photos of prize-winning authors, and posters from previous literary events.

The shelves were crowded with literature, memoirs, poetry, philosophy. There was an absence of cookbooks, self-help and gardening books. Chairs were scattered between shelves, encouraging pausing and reading in the shop.

As the time for the reading evening approached, my courage diminished. There were famous published authors at this conference. Who was I to think I could join this company?

Prairie Lights was in downtown Iowa City. I had noticed a student bar next door when I'd checked out the bookshop earlier. Maybe a couple of pints of local brew would help to settle my nerves. One of

LITERARY MEDICINE

the participants from my workshop accepted my invitation for some pre-reading Dutch courage. Just what the doctor ordered.

We polished off our beers and sauntered to the bookshop as the session was starting. The reading room was packed. There was a podium at the front. The same podium on which Barack Obama had stood not so long ago.

Dave welcomed everyone and introduced the first reader. The list of names of other readers was left on the podium. As each reader finished their piece, they were to call the next reader from this list. No one knew who was going to be next until their name was called.

This was going to be torture.

I sat squirming in the front row. I couldn't pay attention to the pieces being read. But I did notice that most people were reading from books. Their actual books. Not scraps of paper like I had folded in my back pocket. It went on and on. Once we got to about the fifteenth reader, I started to relax a little. Perhaps Dave had forgotten to put my name on the list? He had said there would only be twenty readers. Chances were my name would have been called by now.

I began to doze off. Still feeling the effects of jet lag. And the beers. Through the haze I heard from the podium: 'And the final reader for the night is Hilton Koppe.' Fuck. Shit. Fuck. Where are my pieces of paper? I scrambled to my feet. Thankful the podium hid the pathetic offerings I was clutching.

I looked out at the audience. I was in Iowa City, where medical education shares the stage with stories and emotions, and I was about to jump right in. From the precipice flashed the image of a bumper sticker so popular in Byron Bay, the hippy town near where I live: 'Remember to breathe.'

I took a breath. And read. Two pieces I wrote after my mother's recent death. A short poem and a chaotic piece in response to Derek Mahon's evocative poem, *Everything Is Going to Be All Right*.

ONE CURIOUS DOCTOR

Mother and Son

A mother might imagine that she will …

> Watch her son take his first breath
> Feel his heartbeat for the first time
> Leave hospital with him
> See the sun on his face for the first time
> Carry him into his home
> Buy him nappies
> Wipe his bottom
> See his first smile
> Hear his first words
> See his first steps
> Prepare his first meal
> Sit him on a potty
> Put him on the big toilet
> Teach him how to swallow pills without gagging
> Speak for him at the doctors
> Watch him gain his independence

… And she will do it all with love, each precious moment never, ever forgotten.

A son might never imagine that he will …

> Watch his mum lose her independence
> Speak for her at the doctors
> Teach her how to swallow pills without gagging
> Take her to the toilet on a commode
> Put her on a bed pan
> Clean her incontinence
> Buy her pull-up nappies
> Share her last meal
> See her last steps
> Take her from her home
> See the sun on her face for the last time

LITERARY MEDICINE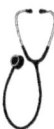

> Bring her to the hospice
> See her final smile
> Hear her final words
> Feel her final pulse
> Watch her take her final breath

… But he will do it all with love, each precious moment never, ever forgotten.

After the Funeral

who the fuck are you to tell me that everything is going to be all right what do you know about my loss you stuck-up self-righteous born-again try-hard excuse for an oracle you may lie below a dormer window whatever the fuck that is I'm prostrated below a ceiling cracked and peeling like the boiled egg that crashed unfelt from my hand this morning yesterday it was a wine glass a wedding gift just last spring from my mother that slipped unbidden from my progressively puerile grip on the world there will be dying you repeat as if it doesn't already have sufficient emphasis maybe you don't need to go into that you're too busy watching the day break I'm witnessing my world break I go into nothing but dying that's all I contemplate your clouds may be clearing mine are gathering not beyond the window they're streaming into this cesspit sucked in by a vacuum of despair uninvited intruders choking the life force out of me you say the sun rises you arrogant arsehole from where I lie the sun is already below the horizon with barely the faintest glow lingering in the western sky the only riot going on here is my battle with the ocean of grief I'm drowning under so don't fucking tell me that everything is going to be all right

I wonder if it is safe to look up. Had my writing managed to span the chasm between modern medicine and humanity?

I lift my gaze from the sweaty ruin of paper in my hands. I see tears. I sense compassion. As I step down from the podium, I am

greeted with words of gratitude. Hugs from strangers. A feeling of belonging. A coming home.

My Iowa experience was neither farcical nor a fly-over. It was the beginning of my journey with words. Plus, I can now dine out on the story that I once shared a podium with Barack Obama!

MAKING IT REAL

SANDRA'S STORY, PART 3

Each year, there is a national medical education conference in Australia. It is a place to showcase innovative educational strategies with peers. I have presented at this conference many times, always striving for something new. Something creative. Something that might unsettle the status quo. Something that challenges me as a presenter as well as challenges the participants. Workshops like 'Pause. Relax. Think deeply. Speak your truth. Using mindfulness in medical education.' Or 'Reclaiming the spirit of medicine – the role of spirituality in medical education.' My offerings were qualitatively different from the usual mainstream fare at the annual conference.

For my next challenge at the education conference, I wanted to share the story of Sandra's involvement in our education program and how it had deepened the learning experience for our students. And to share the ethical challenges of using a patient in education in this way.

I called the session 'Making It Real'. As I began planning the session, I struggled with how to authentically represent Sandra's involvement in our education program. Just telling the story would not do it. How could I make it *really* real? And then it hit me. *Why not ask Sandra if she would be willing to co-present the workshop with me?* Sandra's involvement at our child health workshops has been revelatory. That was just the quality of experience I was hoping to offer for my colleagues at the education conference.

Sandra was initially daunted at the thought of speaking to a group of unknown doctors. She had recently grown relatively relaxed about presenting at our local workshops, and now I was asking her to step out of her comfort zone once again.

Sandra and I came up with a plan to minimise her discomfort. As the interview technique had worked so well at our local workshops, I invited Frank, one of my trusted colleagues who had a deep understanding of the complexities of patient–doctor relationships, to interview Sandra and me. Frank accepted the challenge. He would interview us, and then we would take questions from the audience. This would allow me to be a participant in the story without having to facilitate the event. It would also allow me to maintain a level of care for Sandra, while Frank took care of the audience.

My stated goal for the session was to highlight how Sandra's involvement in our education sessions had helped our learners gain a deeper understanding of the experiences of a parent whose child has a life-threatening illness. But there was a deeper motivation. I wanted to demonstrate the challenges for the patient–doctor relationship which can arise from inviting a current patient to attend as a guest presenter at a medical education session. Most of all, I did want to *make it real*. This meant being open and vulnerable with my emotions and fears. Emotions that came from caring for Sandra and her family. Fears that came from stepping out from the safety of the traditional patient–doctor relationship by inviting Sandra to help with our teaching program.

I wanted to share a poem I had written in response to my first tearful conversation with Sandra years earlier. I told Sandra about the origins of the poem and about my idea to share it during the workshop. 'Would you like to read the poem? We won't use it unless you are happy to do so.'

We agreed that I would email Sandra a copy and hesitantly clicked send. I didn't have to wait long for a reply. Later that afternoon came Sandra's response:

MAKING IT REAL

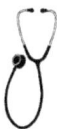

Hi Hilton,

Sometimes the crazy ideas are the ones most worth listening to. The tears I cried by the time I had read to about mid poem were different to the tears I was crying when I read the last line of your poem.

Initially my tears were about the fact that you once again demonstrated your enormous empathy for your patient. This again reinforces for me how much 'you get' what is going on. This is awfully comforting and these days brings me to tears easily when others show empathy (never used to but life experiences change things don't they).

Secondly my tears were about your divulgence of you questioning yourself and your tears. I guess there is something really complex about it like cultural expectations of men and the roles of GPs in our society ... 'GPs should hold it together in front of their patients. Men shouldn't cry, they should be the strong ones otherwise they are weak.' So being a male GP you have a double whammy.

You saw me at my most vulnerable that first appointment. You had courage in abundance when you showed me your vulnerability via your tears. You responded to my pain in a way that allowed me to instantly connect with you and really know I was in fact safe in that room to tell you or say whatever I had to no matter how dark or sad it was. You brought to fruition the message that vulnerability is in fact a strength (not a weakness as most of us have learned to believe) because if you had shut me off with the usual clinical distance that is very common in medical settings, I may not have connected with you that day. Little did you know, I was going out on a limb that day, reaching out to say, 'I have just had six months of clinical, cold, very highly professional staff who never once acknowledged my fear or pain.' I had all my fingers and toes crossed that you would respond to me as a human, acknowledging my struggle.

This is what your tears did, you needed no words. You connected with me as a human.

So Hilton, I did not write this to convince you that you need not question yourself, as you have in the last line of your poem, but to give my perspective of what your tears symbolised for me.

I am blessed to have been referred to you all those years ago.
Sandra :)

It is so rare as a doctor to know, to truly know, whether anything I do really makes a difference to a person. Which person is saved from having a heart attack as a result of my guidance on lowering their blood pressure or cholesterol? Or which person does not get lung cancer because I helped them to stop smoking? Or whether it actually makes a difference when I take the time to explain to my patients how a change in diet and exercise may help prevent diabetes and, if so, which person is the beneficiary of that advice?

But I had made a difference for Sandra.

Sandra, being Sandra, agreed to the poem being read during the workshop. And I, being who I am, thought the poem represented only half of our recent interactions about preparing for the education conference. I was so moved by Sandra's email to me in response to her reading of the poem that I thought it important to include that during the workshop as well, as a rare glimpse into the power of the shared written word. And an even rarer glimpse into the effect that we as doctors can have on our patients.

The power of the poem and the email did not emanate from them being just words on a page. Rather, their power lay in the emotional impact the words brought to the reader, the complex interplay between the writer, the words on a page, and the reader.

The best way to demonstrate this, I thought, was for Sandra to read my poem to the audience, rather than me. I would then read her email in response. This would more closely mimic what happened for each of us during our email exchange. If we were to do it in this way, Sandra's emotional response to my poem may be evident from the way she read it out loud to the workshop participants. And my emotional response to her email would similarly be on show if I read her email. It would make it more real.

I suspected we might find it difficult to contain our emotions if we were to read each other's work. Which is exactly what I hoped the workshop would be able to demonstrate – our real responses to working together through these immensely challenging issues. I

MAKING IT REAL

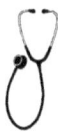

expressed these thoughts to Sandra and, once again, she accepted the challenge. Such trust! In me. In the process.

I sent Frank a copy of Sandra's book to read before the workshop so that he would have a better idea of her story. He would begin the workshop by asking Sandra some questions about the time of diagnosis and initial treatment for Tahlia. He would then invite me to speak a little about becoming involved in the care of Sandra's family. Frank would tease out the intricacies we faced in Sandra becoming involved in our local education workshops. What worked. What was challenging. We would talk about our motivation and rationale for sharing the story of our journey at this workshop. We would be explicit about the challenges of working together as patient and doctor in this way.

At this point in the conversation, Frank would invite Sandra to read my poem about our first conversation. I would then read Sandra's email.

Finally, Frank would ask for questions or comments from the audience. There would be a general discussion about the process we had just shared. There would be rapturous applause.

The audience would throw money. Everything would be all right.

It's always good to have a plan.

Not requiring audiovisual equipment, we have been allocated an open space for our workshop. Not ideal, but we manage to find a fairly quiet and private corner of the conference venue. I arrange for Frank and Sandra to meet beforehand to give us a chance to go over the plan. We are all nervous. And excited. Generally a good sign before a training session.

Ten minutes before we are due to start, people start arriving. Our workshop is part of a much larger conference, and we have no idea how many people are going to come to our session. Five minutes before starting time, all the chairs are full, and we're hunting around for more. Starting time, and the corner of the conference centre is

packed. People are sitting on the floor and standing behind the stairs. Apparently, there is interest in 'Making It Real'.

Frank starts as planned. He does a brilliant job of drawing out Sandra's story. I am watching the reaction of the audience (completely captivated) while at the same time holding Sandra (in the metaphorical way in which a health practitioner supports a patient during challenging times). Sandra shines. She connects with the audience at a deeply personal level. No academic dogma. No guidelines. No graphs. No statistics. Just raw human experience told with dignity and courage.

Then it's my turn. I struggle to know whether to speak directly to Sandra, like 'I remember when we first met', or to talk to the audience and speak about Sandra in the third person. It seems disrespectful to speak about Sandra while she is sitting right next to me, so I direct most of my conversation to Sandra, knowing the audience will understand that I am also speaking to them.

So many thoughts go through my mind as I tell my part of our shared story.

Frank holds the space brilliantly. At precisely the right moment, just as I'm starting to get lost in my thoughts and distracted from the story, he turns to Sandra. 'I understand that Hilton wrote a poem about his reaction to your first conversation. Would you like to read that poem, please Sandra?'

Sandra takes a deep breath. She glances at me. For reassurance or to check if I'm okay, I'm not sure. I nod my support. She begins to read.

MAKING IT REAL

Our First Conversation

You were the one who had been recommended by the cancer care team to see me.
You were the one seeking professional advice.
You were the one seeking professional support.
You were the one who had just returned to our coastal village.
You were the one who had spent months dealing with the massive teaching hospital in the city.
You were the one feeling lost.
You were the one battling the roles of mother and wife and daughter.
You were the one I told 'You don't have to pretend that everything is okay when you come in here.'
You were the one I told 'I want this room to be a sanctuary for you.'
You were the one I told 'You can tell me anything.'
You were the one I told 'There is nothing I can't hear from you.'
You were the one living every parent's nightmare.
You were the one whose daughter had leukaemia.
Why oh why then was I the one to cry?

The words, my words, are no longer scribbles on a page. They are alive. Floating. Flying around us. Reaching to the corners of our small sacred space. Touching the hearts of those listening; those fine doctors who had similar experiences with their own patients, and those who might have been patients.

Sandra's voice quavers. My gaze remains fixed on her. I tell myself that I am focusing my attention on Sandra to support her, as her doctor should. In reality, I am too scared to look up at my peers. My colleagues. How are they reacting? Are they judging me? Is this too weird? Too confronting? I sense the emotion in the room without taking my eyes from Sandra.

Sandra finishes reading. Wipes a tear from her eye. Looks over at me. I nod again. And offer a smile. While all around us, silence.

Frank, the master facilitator, allows us to sit in that silence, understanding its power. Giving us a moment to reflect on what we have just heard.

Just before the silence gets uncomfortable, Frank thanks Sandra and turns to me. 'I understand, Hilton, that when you sent Sandra the poem to read before this workshop, she replied with an email outlining her reaction to your poem. Would you like to read that email for us please?'

I reach for the page containing the email and risk a look at the audience. I see nothing but respect. Support. Love, even. That non-romantic love that good doctors offer the people they care for. I feel held. I feel safe. It gives me courage to go on. Sandra nods reassuringly in my direction.

I begin to read Sandra's email. Slowly. Quietly. Trying to honour her words, as best I can. As I reach the part where Sandra explains the impact my show of emotion had on her that day long ago, it brings me to tears again. At first, I try to fight the tears back. But it's no use. I let go. It feels good. To show how I've been touched by Sandra's response to my humanity. How what I thought could have been a weakness may in fact have been strength. How it is okay to be a doctor and to be human. Just like everyone in the room would like to be able to do.

I finish reading. I wipe the tears from my eyes and face. I look up and allow the audience to come into sharper focus. Tears are flowing everywhere. People are arm in arm, embracing. Offering support and love to each other. To Frank. To Sandra. And to me.

There is no need for applause. Or for the throwing of money.

Love and support are sufficient.

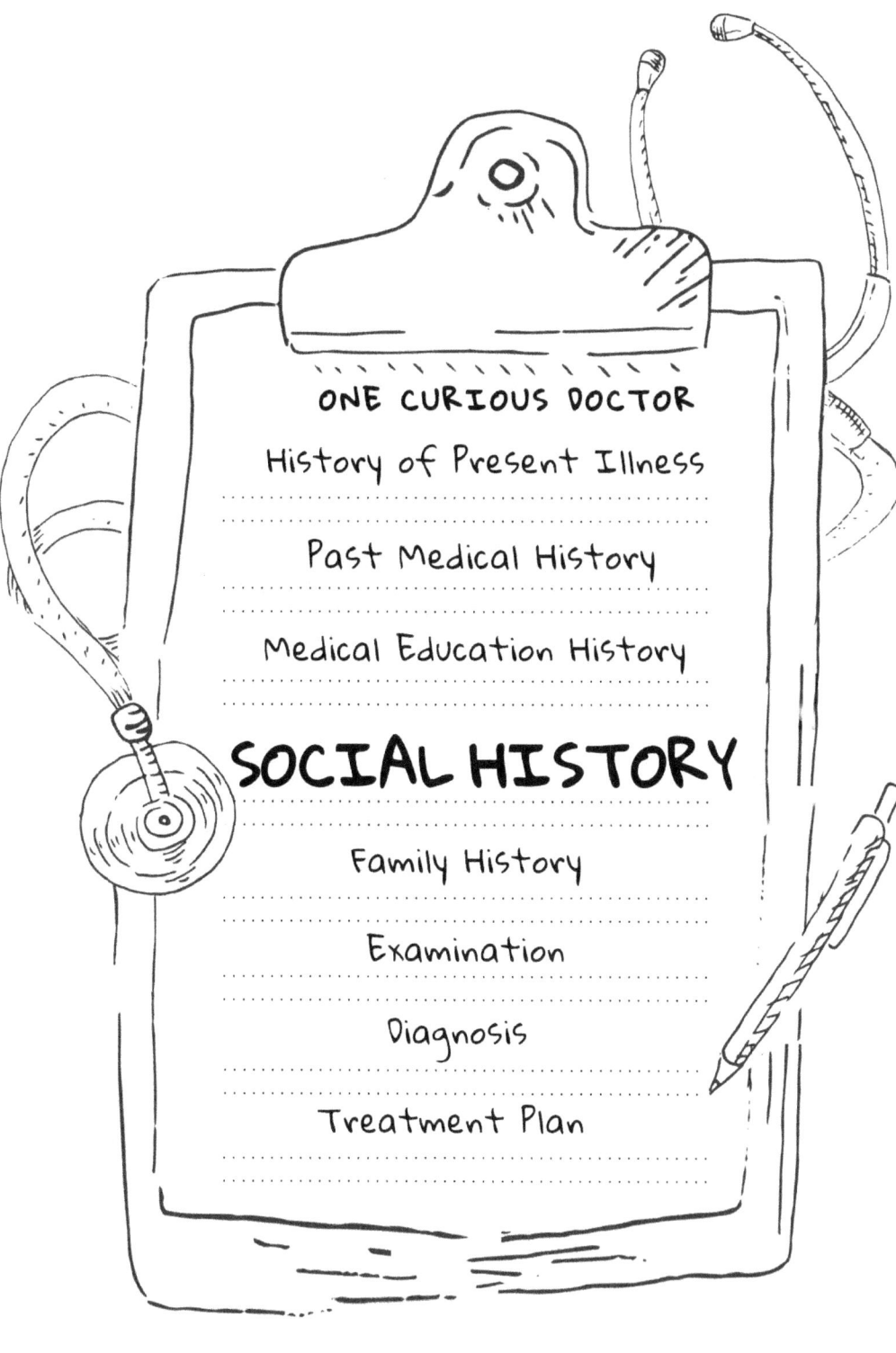

IMAGINING MY OTHER MOTHER

Hilton with Marta, Johannesburg, 1959

Johannesburg, South Africa.
Winter, 1959
Dear Hilton,
As your nanny, I am here for you when you wake up, and I'm here for you while you are asleep. I see you more than I see my own children. I care for you like one of my own. But I know you are not.

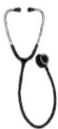

I support you as best as I can while your parents need me. And when they don't need me anymore ... well, I can't bear to think about that.

I live with your family. But I never will be part of your family. I know my place. In time, you will learn your place too. Sadly, there will not be space for you to rest against me, or anyone like me, once that time comes.

Will you remember me? Will you grow up to be kind to my people? Or will you become another one that grinds us down? Treats us like animals?

Take my love with you into the world. My wish is that my love will stay close to your heart so that you will not want to harm my people. I offer this to you freely, even though I am not free.

Be kind and generous, and make the most of your opportunities.

Never ever forget how fortunate you are.

Your other mother,

Marta

Lennox Head, Australia
Spring, 2019
Dear Marta,

I have just discovered this photo from sixty years ago. I guess that you are no longer alive, but I want to thank you for everything you offered me.

What was it like for you? To have to leave your family to live with my family. To care for me instead of your own children. As a father now, I have some understanding of how difficult that must have been.

I am very sorry to say that I have no memory of our time together. It shames me to say this, after everything I imagine that you gave to me. But I was too young when we left South Africa to take memories of you with me, in my conscious mind anyway.

IMAGINING MY OTHER MOTHER

When I saw the photo for the first time a few weeks ago, I was happy to see how happy I looked. I appear so sullen in most other photos from that time. Perhaps it was your presence. I must have felt safe by your side. Did you feel safe being with me? Were you really as relaxed as you look?

Did my father ask you to pose for the photo? Or did he just shoot without asking? There would have been a lot of shooting directed at your people during those years. At least this shot was only with a camera.

I like how we fit together. I like how your arm gently rests against my right thigh, supporting me as I learn to sit.

That area of my thigh is now numb. It happened when my mother was dying nine years ago. I don't know why it became numb then. And I don't know why seeing this photo brought back that memory.

I still crave for the gentle maternal support I lost when my mother died. As must also have happened when we left you in South Africa.

How did your life go after we left? Did you live to see Mandela as president? I hope your family now has something closer to the opportunities I have enjoyed in my life.

I have never ever forgotten how fortunate I am.

With eternal gratitude,

Your other son,

Hilton

DIASPORA BOY

Diaspora Boy asks, 'Where is my home?'

Is it the home of my ancestors?
Is it where I was born?
Is it where I lived the longest?
Is it where I have the most connections?
How will I know when I find my home?

Diaspora Boy asks, 'Could this be my home?'

Hamburg. Birthplace of my father, and his father, and their ancestors. I visited Hamburg in 1984. A stopping-off point on a tour to Scandinavia and Russia. Just one night there, with a visit to the town hall and the Reeperbahn red-light district (looking not buying!). I was twenty-five years old. Too self-centred to ponder what had happened there for my family.

Diaspora Boy asks, 'Could this be my home?'

Mannheim. Birthplace of my father's mother, and her ancestors. I have not been to Mannheim, but in 2009 I attended a conference in Basel in Switzerland. Accompanied by my then eleven-year-old son Liam, *the youngest professor I have ever met*, as one of the other conference delegates described him. Liam and I had dinner one night

at a restaurant overlooking the Rhine River. It triggered a memory of my grandmother talking about her childhood in Mannheim am Rhein. In my imagination, I wondered if any of the molecules of water or rock or weed or moss in the river running by the restaurant had ever been touched by my grandmother. Or other members of her family. Was there something in that river that contained fragments of my DNA?

Diaspora Boy asks, 'Could this be my home?'

Vilnius. The Jerusalem of the north. I visited in 2018 during a trip to the World Cup in nearby Kaliningrad. We approached Vilnius through the birch forests. In my mind's eye, I saw Jews hiding in the shadows, partisans moving through the woods. The birch forests felt familiar. I roamed the streets of Vilnius, walking in the footsteps of my unknown ancestors. And then, after some research, I discovered that my family had lived in small villages hundreds of kilometres from Vilnius. Maybe they had never been there. Or maybe they had.

Diaspora Boy asks, 'Could this be my home?'

Johannesburg. My birthplace and home for the first eighteen months of my life. Refuge for my family en route between Europe and Australia. I don't know our home address, and have no memory of this time. Just a couple of small black-and-white photos. The one I most treasure is of me being held by my African nanny Marta. I don't remember her but the photo shows me that she loved me. Apart from emotions conjured up by this photo, I was devoid of fond feelings for Johannesburg or South Africa. Until the day Nelson Mandela was inaugurated as president. Watching that momentous occasion on television, I was rocked by an unexpected thought. *Maybe it is safe for me to go back now?*

Diaspora Boy asks, 'Could this be my home?'

Bloemfontein. My mother's birthplace. The town where her parents settled when they moved from Lithuania. They lived in a small apartment in a block of flats, ironically called Hilton Mansions. They were anything but mansions. I visited there in 1970 as an eleven-year-old. My *bobba* cooked us *laktes* and *blintzes*, as she had done for my mother when she was a child. Every time I walked past my *zeida*, he would reach out with nicotine-stained fingers to pinch my cheeks – proof that I was really there. These are the only memories I have of my maternal grandparents.

Diaspora Boy asks, 'Could this be my home?'

Paris. I visited there in 1985 as part of my Aussie backpacking pilgrimage through Europe. My father's family had lived in Paris for two years after escaping the Nazis. My grandfather had worked collecting money from vending machines in cafés. He loved Paris. He told me stories of spending his days having a coffee in each café on his rounds. I sat in a Parisian café one sunny spring morning immersed in the echoes of my grandfather's stories. I was surprised by the growing glow of an unusual emotion – belonging. What made me feel so at ease in this foreign city? I wrote an aerogram to my Uncle Steven, a proud Europhile marooned in Australia: 'I think I have fallen in love. It is not with a woman. It is with Europe.'

Diaspora Boy asks, 'Could this be my home?'

Jerusalem. I visited there in search of my source. My origins. As I stood at the Wailing Wall, I wondered how many of my ancestors had stood at the same spot. The lower part of the wall is discoloured from people touching it during their prayers. Were there specks of my DNA in the cracks, along with the notes left by centuries of pilgrims?

Diaspora Boy asks, 'Could this be my home?'

DIASPORA BOY

St Ives. Suburb on the leafy northern outskirts of Sydney. Home during my childhood, adolescence and early adult life. A great place to grow up. Bush across the road, market gardens around us. Until it became overdeveloped suburbia. But I do have a home address: 17 Woodbury Road East. My mother held a farewell party after she sold the house to downsize once her three children had left. She asked me to say a few words. I embarrassed myself by crying as I spoke about our time in our family home. Why was I so emotional about the house being sold? I went back to visit a couple of years later. My mother had told me that the new owners had the house knocked down to build a McMansion. Even though I knew our home would not be there, I did not anticipate the shock of seeing a new building on the block at Woodbury Road. Sitting in the car outside, I felt all the memories from my childhood being scrambled. Something did not compute! It was a most disturbing experience.

Diaspora Boy asks, 'Could this be my home?'

Bangalow. I lived here when I moved from Sydney to become a country doctor. After years of being on the move as a medical student and hospital resident, this was my first chance to live in the same house and work in the same job for six consecutive months. I was thirty years old. I bought my first house in Bangalow. I was married in Bangalow. But I was a European man living in a conservative Australian town. The Shooters Party got the highest number of votes at the Bangalow polling booth during the election just after I had moved there. It was too hot in summer and too cold in winter. No, I'm sure this isn't my home.

Diaspora Boy asks, 'Could this be my home?'

Lennox Head. Where I now live. Where I now work. Where my children have grown up. Where we built our home. Where I have planted a garden. Where I have community. Where there are so many stories. Where I am so happy. Could this be my home?

ONE CURIOUS DOCTOR

My DNA might answer, *No, home is elsewhere.*

But my head says, *Yes, this is home!*
My heart says, *Yes, this is home!*
My family says, *Yes, this is home!*
The trees in the garden say, *Yes, this is home!*

Finally, Diaspora Boy finds home.

SLICE OF LIFE

In my late twenties, I sought a path toward my authentic self. I'd done all that had been scripted for someone like me. Did well at high school. Graduated from medical school at the wise old age of twenty-three. Worked at a Sydney hospital for two years. I'd done the Aussie backpacker stint in Europe. Worked in emergency departments in England for couple of years. Returned to Sydney to complete my general practice training. Did three months during my training as a country doctor in Coffs Harbour, a small town eight hours drive and a world away from Sydney.

I was fulfilling every Jewish parent's dream for their son (the doctor). But I felt lost. Alone. Existentially bereft.

I thought maybe I'd be better off if I returned to Coffs Harbour. I'd met some interesting people there. People who believed in the healing power of yoga and meditation. Not drugs and surgery. They opened my eyes to new possibilities. I learnt to be more flexible with my mind and my body. Once I was even able to touch my toes. Adarsha, the yoga teacher, told me how this was a rare feat for someone who thinks as much as I do.

One of my friends worked for the tax office during the week and dabbled as a clairvoyant on weekends. For my thirtieth birthday she offered me a free healing session. She told me that I was experiencing an archetypal reaction to my Saturn's return, which apparently is some sort of astrological phenomenon. She said that if I wanted to

be by the ocean and under the trees, then I should go and live by the ocean and under the trees. It was there I would find my soulmate. Not by the Opera House or under The Bridge.

I took the plunge and followed the clairvoyant's advice.

This middle-class pilgrimage of privilege led me to a rebirthing workshop in the Byron Bay hinterland. I spent a week with a gaggle of dishevelled anaemic soul-seekers, you know, the kind who frequent health food shops and don't believe much in deodorant. We were guided in techniques designed to transport us to our past lives and thus offer insight into our higher selves. What the process actually involved was lying down and hyperventilating to the point where the carbon dioxide in our brains plummeted to levels that induced hallucinations.

It was fun.

During one of these psychotomimetic trances, I regressed and re-experienced the days after my birth. For the first week, I delighted in my family showering me with joy and love and peace and happiness. And then, on the eighth day, my foreskin was hacked off. Pain and confusion followed as those who had previously showered me with joy and love and peace and happiness sang hymns of gratitude in response to my defilement. As they celebrated and I screamed, I felt as disconnected from those around me as my foreskin was from its former spiritual home.

Post this rebirthing experience, I began contemplating what might have happened to my foreskin. Was it disposed of in a ritual manner? Jews do not practise cremation, so I suspect it wasn't burnt. Did it get buried? Like a placenta may be interred under a favourite tree. Was it offered to my parents in a yellow-lidded plastic jar like a gallstone after its removal? Was it binned and, if so, did it go into the green bin for composting or the red bin for landfill? I hope it wasn't recycled, as foreskins are in the Yiddish folktale about the rabbi's wife who used the off cuts from circumcisions to make magical purses that became tumescent with gentle stroking.

SLICE OF LIFE

I have wondered how different life may have been if my foreskin remained where God (surely) intended it to be. Would I have been at greater risk of HIV and other sexually transmitted infections, as the pro-cut lobby claims? Or would my sexual experiences have been heightened, as suggested by the anti-cutters?

I lost many things during my childhood. My African nanny disappeared suddenly from my life when we migrated to Australia. My beloved Teddy's head dropped off on my seventh birthday. My illusion of belonging to a happy family evaporated when my parents divorced.

Is it okay to add my foreskin to the list of childhood losses to mourn?

WHAT IF I'D LISTENED TO MY HEART?

What I dreamt of as a teenager.

To play soccer for Australia at the World Cup.

What I dreamt of as a young adult.

To play soccer for Australia at the World Cup.

What I dreamt of in middle age, when I should have been old enough to know better.

To play soccer for Australia at the World Cup. Some things never change.

What happened in early 2014.

I got selected to play soccer for Australia at the World Cup in Brazil. In the national team for Australian doctors. The Master Docceroos. At the World Medical Soccer Championship being held in Brazil during *the* World Cup.

What this meant to me.

The world. A dream come true.

What I did to prepare.

Got fit. Really fit. Lost nearly 10 kg. Joined a slipper camp – a boot camp for old blokes.

WHAT IF I'D LISTENED TO MY HEART?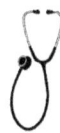

What difference this made.

Heaps. My soccer improved. I started playing the best soccer of my life. At age fifty-five. And I loved it.

What the Master Docceroos did to prepare.

Planned a few training sessions. Entered a couple of masters tournaments together. This was not easy to arrange as we came from all over Australia.

What I felt before our first training session.

Nervous. Really nervous. I so desperately wanted to fit in. Socially. And on the field. I didn't want to be a burden in either way.

What I felt after the first training session.

Exhausted – it was a hot Sydney day in February. Exhilarated – the other blokes made me feel very welcome. And it looked like my soccer skills would be okay after all.

What I felt after our first tournament.

Exhausted – five games in two days in unseasonably hot March weather. Exhilarated – got to know the other guys much better.

What else I felt after our first tournament.

Hungover.

What I arranged for the July long weekend.

For the Master Docceroos to play a tournament in Bangalow, near to where I live.

What I felt in the lead up to the Bangalow tournament.

Excited. To be welcoming my new friends to my home turf. To play together again. To share a couple of meals again.

What my heart said on the way to my local club game the week before the Bangalow tournament.

Bump … Bump … Bump**BUMP** … Bump… Bump … Bump**BUMP**

What I thought when this happened.

That's weird. I've never felt that before. I wonder what that's all about? I wonder if maybe I shouldn't play?

What I did about it.

Nothing. Ignored it. I may be a doctor, but first and foremost, I am a middle-aged Australian man, hard wired to ignore things like this. So, I played. Stupidly.

What happened during the first half of the game.

Nothing. With my heart. Felt fine all through the first half.

What happened during the second half of the game.

Nothing. With my heart.

What else happened.

I got hit by a bad tackle. A really bad tackle. A studs-up sliding tackle. Got me in my left ankle. With so much force it broke the skin through my shin pads.

What I felt.

Not much pain. Surprisingly. Considering how hard he hit me.

What else I felt.

Rage. At the danger he put me in with such an unnecessarily vicious tackle.

What I said.

You prick. You fucking prick. Coming in like that.

What the ref said to me.

Shut up. Move away.

What the ref did.

WHAT IF I'D LISTENED TO MY HEART?

Gave the other player a yellow card.

What I said.

You're joking. A yellow card for a tackle like that. What a joke.

What my teammates said.

Shut up, Hilton. Move away.

What I felt when I moved away.

My knee wobble.

What I knew then.

My medial collateral ligament was torn.

What I felt next.

Pissed off. Really pissed off. Like really, really pissed off. Probably more pissed off than I could remember.

What I knew then.

That the dream could be over.

What I should have done.

Listened to my heart before the game. There have been no palpitations since.

What I did when I got home.

Tested the ligaments in my knee as best as I could.

What those tests told me.

That my medial collateral ligament was torn.

What I did next.

Cried.

What I did then.

Googled medial collateral ligament injuries. As I had feared, recovery

time would not be long enough for me to be fit to play in Brazil.

What started at that moment.

The roller-coaster ride. *Yes, I can do this, I'll be right ... No, this is hopeless, I'll never be right in time ... Yes, I can do this, I'll be right ... No, this is hopeless, I'll never be right in time ...*

What I did on Monday morning.

Asked my colleague to examine my knee.

What he said.

Your medial collateral ligament is torn.

What I did next.

Arranged to have an MRI scan of my knee the next evening.

What the MRI machine said.

JACK JACK JACK JACK JACK JACK JACK

What Bob Dylan sang through the headphones given to me to try to drown out the jackhammering of the MRI machine.

Don't Think Twice, It's All Right.

What I did.

Tried not to think twice, so that it would be all right. This was not easy.

What the radiographer said after the scan.

Looks like your ligament is definitely torn.

What my sleep was like that night.

Terrible. It's hard to sleep when you're on a roller coaster.

What the physio said when I saw him the next day.

It will be difficult to recover in time to play in Brazil. You risk catastrophic injury if you play.

WHAT IF I'D LISTENED TO MY HEART?

What my GP said.

It will be difficult to recover in time to play in Brazil. You risk catastrophic injury if you play.

What my Master Docceroos teammates said via email.

You'll be right, Hilton. Do your rehab. See you on the weekend in Bangalow.

What it was like watching them play in Bangalow.

Terrible. It was great to see them. And to act as coach. To make the substitutions. But watching them and not being able to play. It was terrible.

What I said to them.

I don't know if I'm going to come to Brazil if I can't play.

What they said.

You'll be right, Hilton. Do your rehab. See you in Brazil.

What I realised when I thought deeply about the decision I needed to make.

Maybe it's better to not go and to be disappointed for a short time than to go, have a catastrophic injury, and then have major regrets.

What a friend said to me when I asked him for advice.

It's a no-brainer Hilton.

What my wife said to me when I asked her for advice.

It's a long way to go, Hilt. To watch other people living your dream.

What my knee did when I got out of bed the next morning.

Gave way.

What I did that day.

Cancelled my trip.

What I did instead of going with my son to Brazil.

Took my son on a three-week bodyboarding road trip in Australia. His dream had always been to go on a bodyboarding road trip with me. At least his dream could come true.

What the road trip was like.

Awesome. A totally awesome time for both of us.

What I regret about this whole experience.

Nothing.

What I gained from this experience.

The opportunity to reflect on how I want to make decisions in my life.

What I lost from this experience.

Nearly 10 kg.

What I learnt from this experience.

Jump. When someone comes sliding in for a tackle.

What else I learnt from this experience.

Listen. When my heart is trying to tell me something.

What my dream was next.

To play soccer for Australia at the World Cup in Russia in 2018. Some things never change.

WHERE DREAMS MEET DELUSIONS

I was a boy of modest dreams. My grandpa's tales of failed aspirations had taught me that. *Träume klein. Enttäuschung vermeiden.* Dream small. Avoid disappointment. The philosophy of Grandpa's convoluted life condensed into bumper-sticker wisdom.

So my childhood dreams were simple. While other kids spoke of their desires for their family to get a swimming pool or a Chrysler Charger, I silently wished for summer holidays with cousins just like the Aussie kids. Or of being accepted equally on the Kingpin court with the boys and playing elastics with the girls. Or of quietly fitting in without being invisible.

During adolescence, my dreams evolved into visions so grand that there was no chance of them ever happening. An equally good way to avoid disappointment. My grandfather would have been proud. My classmates dreamt of being seduced by unattainable older girls. Or being the next Ringo Starr. I dreamt of conscription being abolished in Australia before I was old enough for my birthdate to be pulled from the ballot. Bizarrely for a thirteen-year-old, I also aspired to be Secretary General of the United Nations.

I did manage to squeeze in one or two dreams that might be considered normal for a wannabe Aussie teenager. I yearned to emulate the exploits of my larrikin fan-boy heroes like the Australian cricketers Dennis Lillee and Rod Marsh. Until a Jimmy Mackay right foot bullet into the back of the South Korean goal catapulted the

Australian soccer team to their first ever World Cup appearance in 1974. I became obsessed with a vision of one day playing soccer for Australia. I was going to be a Socceroo!

I loved playing soccer. It was the place where I finally fitted in. My teammates felt like real friends, unlike my classmates, who preferred to use me as a punching bag. But Grandpa didn't need to worry that I was aiming too high; I was one of the lesser players in an average team. No chance of ever being part of an Australian team at the World Cup. A safe unattainable dream.

Forty years later, when I was selected to play in the Australian doctor's soccer team at the World Medical Football Championships, my safe unattainable dream had become a risky reality.

But my medial collateral ligament stayed true to my grandpa's foreboding. *Träume klein. Enttäuschung vermeiden.* Dream small. Avoid disappointment. I was learning the lesson the hard way!

However, in time I did recover from the knee injury, and was able to make the subsequent Master Docceroos team for the 2015 World Medical Football Championship. I was about to become the oldest and least skilful player ever to wear the green and gold of an Australian soccer team.

My first game for Australia was against Lithuania, the home of my mother's family and the resting place of my ancestors, many of whom had been killed for being Jewish during the recurring conflicts in that region. I was looking forward to a comradely game. Perhaps against descendants of long-lost family members, or distant cousins.

The build-up to the game was an emotional experience. I was living my dream. Could my grandfather have been wrong? Maybe dreaming big was a better way to live my life.

I wasn't the only one basking in the delight of big dreams. One of the psychiatrists in our team described us as 'a mob of intelligent adults all sharing the same delusion that we are actually international footballers'.

Despite the psychiatric cynicism, I found myself holding back tears as I was presented with my baggy green cap, in the tradition of players making their debut for the Australian cricket team.

WHERE DREAMS MEET DELUSIONS

The moment I was most excited about was not far away – the playing of the national anthems. For decades I had fantasised about standing side by side, shoulder to shoulder, with my Australian teammates, belting out the words of 'Advance Australia Fair' before going into battle against a foreign enemy. I had witnessed this on TV so many times. It was about to be my turn.

As we lined up in front of a crowd made up entirely of encouraging wives and kids, I was struck by the dourness of the Lithuanians. I was like a puppy with a new ball. They looked like they were going to a funeral. My impressions appeared to be confirmed when the first national anthem was played, a typically dour European dirge, and the Lithuanians didn't sing. *Oh well, their loss. It's not going to stop me from going my hardest when it's our turn to sing.*

After fifty-six years of waiting for this moment, I took a deep breath, readying myself for 'Australians all, let us rejoice ...' The opening bars of the anthem played. It was an unusual opening. Not like any intro melody I'd heard before. I'm about to burst into song when the Lithuanians start singing. It's their anthem. Not ours. What the hell is going on? The moment I'd been waiting for. Gone. Just like Grandpa said.

We learnt later that the organisers had made a mistake. They had played the Austrian anthem in place of ours.

As we shook hands with the Lithuanians after the anthems, the next disappointment was upon me. No smiles, no eye contact, no 'Have a good game' as we walked down their ranks. They had hands like no doctor I knew. Thick gnarly fingers. My hands were like a cashmere scarf compared to their leathery palms. They were the hands of men who knew how to handle physical demands. A shovel. An axe. God knows what else. Was I imagining it, or did they also have a blood lust in their eyes?

They were hard men who I guessed had lived hard lives. And that was how they played. As if their lives depended on it. We might have been the more skilful team, but we didn't stand a chance against their physical intimidation.

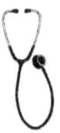

ONE CURIOUS DOCTOR

During a few moments on the sidelines after being subbed off for a breather, a most disturbing thought intruded into my delusional mind. *These are not the descendants of my long-lost relatives, these are the descendants of those who killed my long-lost relatives.*

It was hard to focus on soccer after that. We lost the match.

But they did allow us to sing our national anthem at the end of the game. After I cheekily explained to the embarrassed organisers, 'We are the other Austria, you know, the big island Austria in the middle of the Pacific Ocean!'

It had been a momentous day for me. I had ticked off two big dreams in one day – playing for Australia and singing the national anthem shoulder to shoulder with my teammates. I wonder what Grandpa's advice about dreams would be now? And I wonder about how I might advise my grandchildren in the future? *Träume groß. Reue vermeiden.* Dream big. Avoid regrets. Perhaps it's not too late for me to start following this philosophy too.

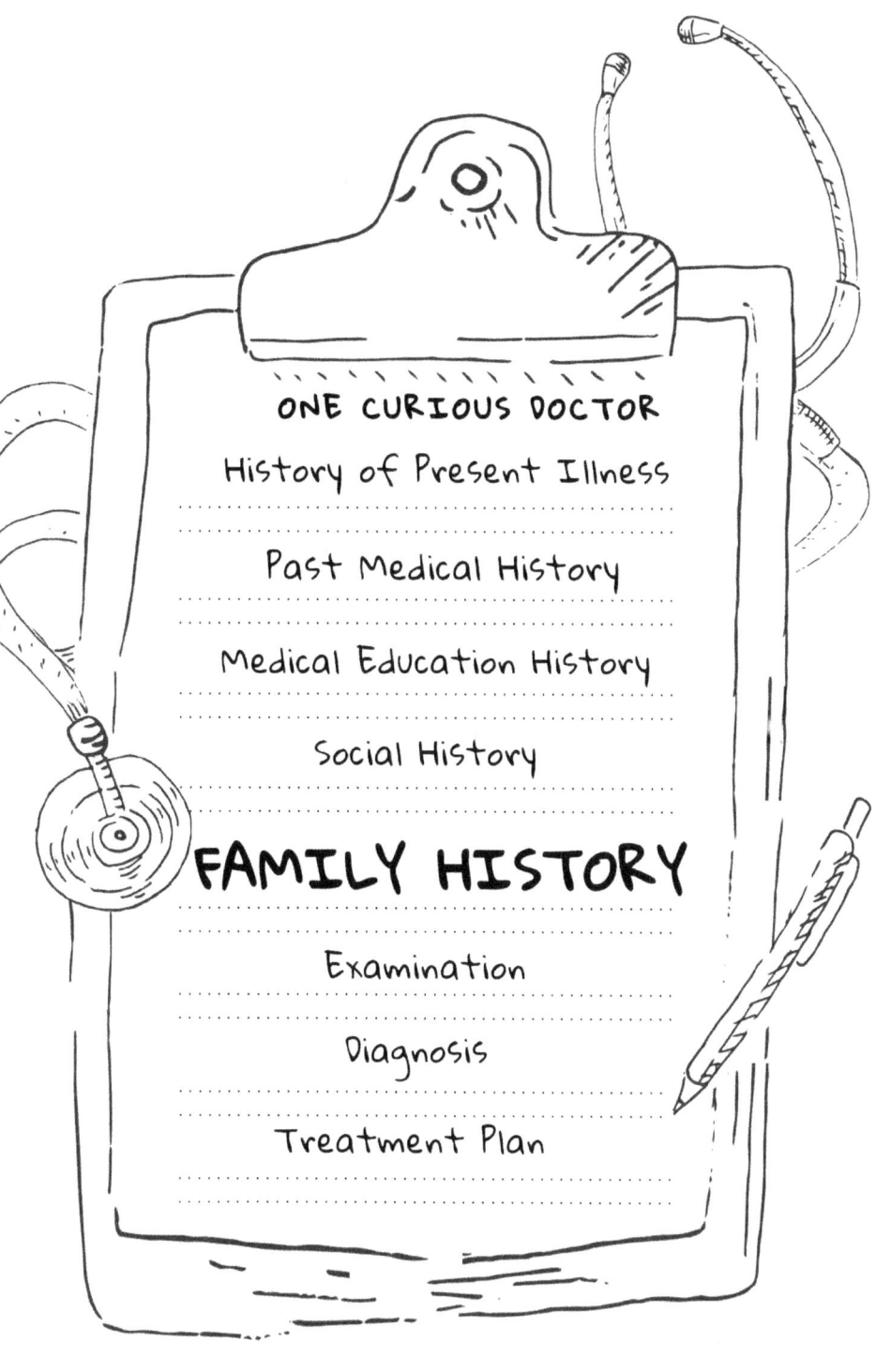

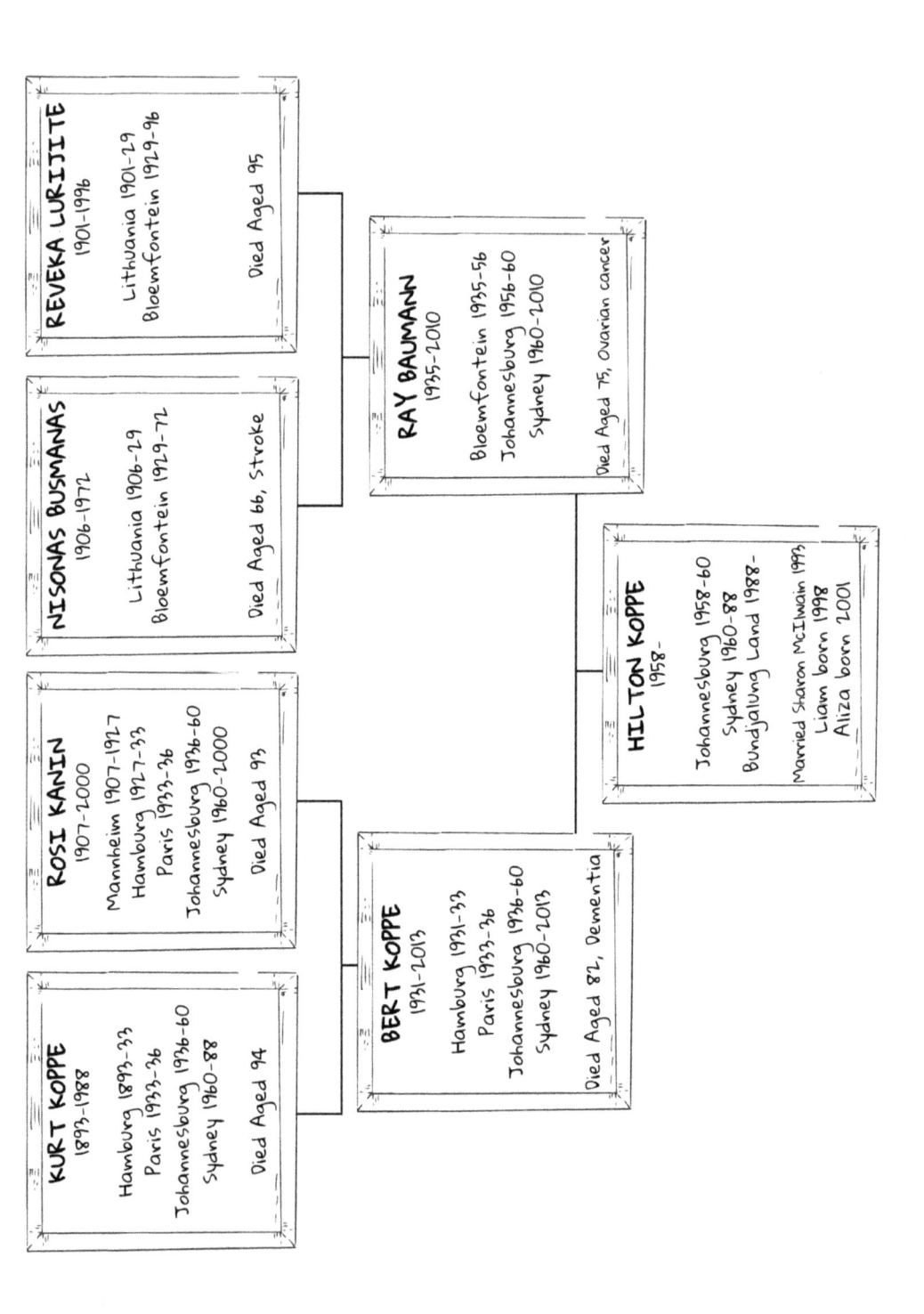

Wedding of Hilton's parents, Johannesburg, 1956.

From L to R: Nisonas Bauman (formerly Busmanas), Reveka Bauman (nee Lurijite), David Bauman, Ray Bauman, Bert Koppe, Stephen Koppe, Rosi Koppe (nee Kanin), Kurt Koppe

IGNORING VITAL SIGNS

Since I moved from the city to work as a country doctor twenty-five years ago, I see my mum less often. But I see her better. She visits a few times a year and stays for a week or more. We get to share breakfast, lunch and dinner.

Tonight, I am sitting with her in our lounge room. My kids are in bed. My wife is out. It is just the two of us watching *Fiddler on the Roof*. 'You know, this story of Tevye and Golde is the story of our family. My parents would have grown up in a *shtetl* very similar to this in Lithuania before they escaped to South Africa. That's why we're alive. Unlike the rest of the village who stayed,' she confides in a whisper that screams of survivor's guilt.

I gaze across to Mum. Stubble of grey hair sprouting from her near-bald scalp. Moon face from the steroids she's taking to reduce the side effects of chemotherapy.

This is Mum's fourth dance with cancer. The first came not long after I'd left Sydney. Breast cancer. She needed surgery. Radiotherapy. Chemotherapy. The second cancer, two years later. Bony secondaries. Bad outlook. More chemotherapy and radiotherapy. A good outcome. A miracle.

Later, a new breast cancer in the same breast that had received all that radiotherapy fifteen years earlier. That time, it was mastectomy and more chemotherapy.

And now, ovarian cancer.

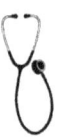

How did Mum manage to survive so many cancers? Perhaps it was her positive attitude. 'I know how to beat this damn cancer,' she declared with her first diagnosis. 'I'll just have lots of Hannah therapy. That'll do the trick.' Hannah was her first grandchild. Mum used to drive across Sydney once or twice a week to hang out with Hannah. She'd take her to the park on sunny days. Or sit and play with her on the floor. My brother told me that sometimes she just sat by Hannah's cot while she slept, in silent communion with her granddaughter. And perhaps with the ghosts of her family too.

As successive grandchildren arrived, her love for them, and love for her children and friends, must have helped Mum in her drive to survive.

I believe there is something in addition to love that explained her survival. Throughout her long journey with cancer, Mum always had trust in her medical team. Complete trust. Faith.

She had quite a team. Nurses. Surgeons. Family medicine practitioners. Radiologists. Pharmacists. Her oncologist for over twenty years who remained optimistic and guided Mum towards recovery when perhaps a good outcome was not expected. 'I always knew your mum would do well,' the oncologist once told me. 'I could tell from the moment I met her that she was going to be a survivor.'

Mum had complete faith in them all. Could it have been that this faith was a significant factor in her capacity to recover from the unrecoverable?

Research suggests that people with religious faith have better medical outcomes than non-believers. So why not faith in the medical team? Could that aid survival in a similar way to religious faith?

Mum cared for her medical team at least as much as they cared for her. She was that kind of woman. She would often tell me how tired her oncologist was looking, or of the worries her current family doctor was having with her children. My guess is that they all benefited as much from seeing Mum as she did from seeing them.

IGNORING VITAL SIGNS

Just before her surgery for ovarian cancer, Mum notices a lump in her groin. She asks her family doctor about it, and is told it might be a small hernia. The oncological gynaecologist checks it out just before doing Mum's radical hysterectomy and says that she doesn't think it is anything to worry about. I am with Mum when she tells her oncologist about the lump at a planning visit prior to commencing chemotherapy. I hear the oncologist say from behind the curtain, 'That might be a small lymph gland. We should just keep an eye on it.'

A lymph gland in the groin! In a woman who had just been under the knife for ovarian cancer! I decode the specialist's doctor-speak. The cancer might have spread. Has the oncologist just uttered Mum's death sentence?

Somehow, I manage to contain my terror. I resist becoming an interfering medical son. Was I overreacting? Or had I become infected with Mum's faith in her medical team?

The day before her chemotherapy treatment is due to start, Mum phones me. 'That lump in my groin is getting bigger. And more painful. It's starting to really worry me.'

I could sit on my hands no longer. 'Mum, you need to get an urgent appointment for an ultrasound of your groin. And to delay the chemotherapy until the results of the ultrasound are available.'

She phones the next day to read me the ultrasound report. I translate the medical jargon. 'Mum, what that's saying is that the lump in your groin is probably a secondary cancer.'

My unspoken fears have just found a voice. The doctor part of my brain was screaming, 'This is the beginning of the end!' The rest of my brain yelled, 'How could this happen? How could so many good doctors have fucked up so bad? It shouldn't be up to a son to diagnose his mum's cancer from 800 kilometres away.'

I tried to imagine what might have been going on for Mum's doctors. How could they fail to act on such a potentially important sign? Was it because they were set on the plan they already had in mind? Did

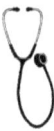

they think that it was the job of one of the other team members to follow up on this? Were they too busy or too tired to take what they knew would be a more challenging path?

Or could it have been that Mum was too likable for her own good. Were her doctors afraid of the potential consequences of these symptoms? Did their attachment to Mum make it impossible for them to contemplate yet another cancer? Was the thought of that too much for them to stomach?

I thought about how I react with my own patients. It is easy to remember the times I have made errors because I was angry with the people I was supposed to be caring for. Like the time I missed a diagnosis of acute kidney failure in a middle-aged man because he had so many annoying habits. Or the time I failed to diagnose a case of appendicitis because I was resentful having to do a house call to see the young boy when I thought his mother should have brought him to the clinic. And I think about times when I have been so busy or tired that I have chosen a path of least resistance. An easy path in the short term, but not ultimately the correct path.

But what about the opposite? How do I react with my special patients, like those with whom I have shared decades-long journeys through sickness and health? Or with patients who are parents of my friends? Patients who are classmates of my children or who are fellow soccer players? Patients who are colleagues? How often have there been times when my personal attachment to a patient resulted in me being unable or unwilling to bear the potential consequences of a worrying symptom? Have I been guilty of ignoring vital signs? No doubt I have.

Mum's ovarian cancer is aggressive. She quickly deteriorates. We organise for her to see a professor on the other side of Sydney. He is doing a drug trial for women with a specific genetic abnormality that makes them more likely to get breast and ovarian cancer. His patients are mostly Eastern European Jewish women. Sitting in his waiting room with Mum is a sobering experience. I can't help but think of

IGNORING VITAL SIGNS

Auschwitz. Bald emaciated women at the mercy of someone using experimental protocols to decide their fate.

But this doctor is an angel. Not a Mengele. Generous with his time. Thoughtful. Understanding. Kind. The experimental drug (and its prescriber) offers hope. But not good results.

Too soon, Mum is in the palliative care hospice. I am with her as she listens carefully to the doctor who is explaining how they will take care of her needs – physical, emotional and spiritual. She asks a few questions which are answered patiently. At the end of the conversation, Mum reaches for the doctor's hand. She gently strokes the back of the doctor's arm as she thanks her for making her feel so much better. Right to the end, Mum is still taking care of others.

My last patient before lunch is Liz. I see her sitting in the waiting room. Stubble of grey hair sprouting from her near bald scalp. Moon face from the steroids she's taking to reduce the side effects of chemotherapy.

I had discovered Liz's uterine cancer a year ago as part of a routine check-up. She's had surgery and chemotherapy. All is going well. She had follow-up tests last week and is coming in for the results.

'Liz,' I say before we have even sat down, 'the results are fantastic. Your tumour markers are undetectable and there's no sign of cancer on the scans.'

She bursts into tears with this news. 'Thank you for saving my life,' she gushes.

If only I could have done that for my mum, I silently cry. If only.

BEARING WITNESS

I had only ever seen one person die. I mean, really seen them die. Last gasp and all that. Thirty years of doctoring and witness to only one death. Until now. Now it is two.

Not that I'm some sort of demi-god super-doc whose patients never die. Of course my patients die. For some, I had the privilege of midwifing them on their final journey. For others, it was all too sudden and unexpected. But though I saw their struggle with life, I never saw them die.

For each of these, I tried to stem the tide, swim against the rip, keep my finger in the dyke, spit into the wind, push the shit uphill. But as my wise grandmother used to say, *'Mein lieber Gott vergisst niemanden.'* My dear God forgets no one. Despite my best efforts and the magic of modern medicine, Nature still has her victory in the end.

There were the timed and documented moments of death in hospitals. The failed resuscitations. But did I see these people actually die? I don't think so. They were already dead by the time the emergency pager went off. We could not bring them back to life. They were not Lazarus. We were not God. I did not witness them die. I saw them fail to rise. Doctors 0 – Nature 1. Again and again.

Rod Stewart was belting out 'The First Cut Is the Deepest' around the time I was cut by a last breath for the first time. I was on night shift, the solitary junior resident on a male medical ward. James Ward.

BEARING WITNESS

Spit Alley, we called it. Full of public patients, not-for-resuscitation veterans in the days when ANZAC diggers were still alive.

Then, I was a young sapling with no firm grounding in the bedrock of medicine.

I was scared. Shit scared.

At 6 pm, they all go. The day staff. The senior residents. My fellow juniors. Leaving me alone with the nurses and with the enemy, our defensive moniker for the patients.

The pager bleats. An admission from Emergency. 'We've got an old guy with anaemia. Probable bleeding ulcer. We're sending him up.'

I enter the ward. Grab his file. Draw back the curtain that separates him from the thirty other inmates on James Ward. I am confronted by a ghost of a man, scarecrow hair, chest-length beard, pallid face, dinner-plate eyes. He greets me with a deep guttural moan. Reaches out a desperate hand. And dies. Despite all my training and the mythology of doctor as hero, there is not a damned thing I can do about it.

His final breath. My first death.

Thirty years later, I was witness to a second death. It was not a patient this time. It was my mum. I was with her on the palliative care ward. No longer a doctor pushing shit uphill, but a son assisting Nature to do her thing.

And Mum was remarkable. Such grace. Such dignity in her dying, just as in her life. She was ready to die. Not afraid of death. Exhausted after twenty years of treatment for breast cancer and then terminal ovarian cancer. She was sad to be leaving her family. But ready to go. Definitely ready to go.

She had said goodbye to her home. She had said goodbye to her friends. She had said goodbye to my sister who lived overseas and to all her grandchildren. She even said goodbye to her oncologist, who had walked with her for two decades. 'I hope you don't feel that I'm letting you down by dying, after everything you have done for me.'

I was blessed to be with her at the end. As her breath was

transformed. From laboured grunting to soft sucking. Slowing. Easing.

Which was her final breath? The last inhalation? Or that explosive sigh a few moments later? It scared the life out of me as Mum's body relaxed completely for the first time in her life.

I sat and silently encouraged her to let go. Bearing witness to the end of a good life.

In loving memory of Ray Koppe,
28/02/1935—24/09/2010

'Our Ray of sunshine, forever in our hearts.'

DENIAL IMPOSSIBLE

I was being the archetypal annoying medical relative blowing in from out of town with (unrealistic, as they turned out to be) demands of the medical and nursing staff caring for my father. He had been admitted to hospital the previous week after four falls within a few days. These falls came on the back of progressive decline in memory and mobility since turning eighty a year earlier.

I had rushed to finish work in time to catch the evening flight to Sydney, and spent a restless night in a hotel trying to imagine the sight of my father in a hospital bed. Dad had previously been quite healthy. This was going to be the first time I had ever visited him in a hospital. Compounding my anticipatory anxiety, he had been admitted to the hospital where I had worked as a resident thirty years before. Here was where my adolescence ended. Being my first visit back to the site of my initiation into the family of medicine, many memories resurfaced, some of them unpleasant. All of them unwelcome. I had enough to focus on without being thrown back to my turbulent past.

Dad was in a hospital gown, sporting a black eye from one of his falls. *My old man now looks like an old man!* There is nothing like a hospital gown to make denial impossible.

His face lit up as he saw me approach. At least that spark had not yet been extinguished. But the full extent of his decline over the six weeks since I had last seen him quickly became apparent. It was not possible to hold his attention to a conversation for more than a few

moments. He was easily distracted by what was going on in the ward. I'd let him have these mental wanders and then gently bring him back to our conversation, sometimes needing to start over.

I asked him about his understanding of why he was in hospital. He knew it was because he had been falling. He wanted to have treatment and then go home. This was my wish too.

Dad wasn't invited to the meeting with his medical team. His partner and her daughter were there. My sister was on the speakerphone from New York. There were two doctors, the nurse unit manager, and a social worker who I suspected hadn't been born when I last worked at the hospital.

The social worker got things started. 'Your dad has been assessed by the team. We have determined that he is high care because of his dementia and physical frailty. He needs to be in an institution where this level of care can be safely managed. We don't think it's appropriate for him to go home and, therefore, we cannot offer him rehab.'

That bombshell was their opening gambit and no amount of probing or encouraging or beseeching on my behalf was able to shift their position. 'You know that this will kill him,' was my final plea.

Despite my delusion that I have the power to talk people round to my way of thinking, I was unable to do that for my father. The team listened well. They understood. But they did not change their minds. I wondered if they were on the same team as us.

His partner was heartbroken. She wanted to be able to care for Dad at home, but the staff warned her how difficult that would be and she rightly accepted their advice. She couldn't face telling him. I said that I would do it. Years of experience at breaking bad news to my patients provided little consolation. Another life-stage transition was about to take place within these hospital walls.

I held my dad's hand. I cried as I explained to him what the hospital staff had said. That they felt there was little chance of him getting better.

DENIAL IMPOSSIBLE

Dad listened. My rare show of emotional affection and the life-changing news accompanying it were able to hold his attention for more than a few moments. Then he surprised me.

'Well, I guess it could be worse.'

'Worse! What could possibly be worse than this?'

'At least I'm not dying.'

DUET FOR THE DEAD

I am sitting in my father's hospital room.

We gather around his deathbed. My younger brother stands and soothes our dad with calm words, stroking his hair as a father would for a child having difficulty getting to sleep. My father's partner sits by his side, nudging him awake every time his breathing slows, not yet ready to let him go. I sit in the corner. Holding everyone in my heart.

In this moment, I wonder, *Who is going to hold me?*

I am sitting in the front pew at my father's funeral.

The rabbi's voice drones on in a foreign tongue. I try to glean meaning from these guttural sounds, but it's an effort to find salve in these incomprehensible prayers. The rabbi nods to me. The eldest son. I step forward. As tradition demands. The rabbi cuts the tip off my tie. Something has been severed. That will never be the same again.

In this moment, I feel cleaved.

I am standing by my father's grave.

The rabbi's voice drones on in a foreign tongue. He nods to me. The eldest son. I step forward. As tradition demands. He passes me the shovel. I brace myself for this moment. Now, I am the head of my family. I need to show strength. I fill the shovel with clods of earth. I toss the earth into the grave. Onto the coffin. With more force than necessary. The sound reverberates in my head. And in my heart.

In this moment, I feel lighter.

DUET FOR THE DEAD

I am walking with my family away from my father's grave.

The path is flanked by my father's friends. As tradition demands. Many are faces from my childhood. Some are just names from stories. They usher us away from death. Toward life. Each person offers me their hand. And the ritual greeting, 'I wish you a long life.'

In this moment, I feel held.

I am sitting in the synagogue.

It is my first attendance since my brother's bar mitzvah more than forty years before. That day, as the time for my reading approached, my father put his arm around me. An offering of encouragement. And a rare moment of meaningful connection. Today, the congregation for the evening service is swelled by my father's mourners. The rabbi nods to my brother and me. As tradition demands. We stand. Side by side. Shoulder to shoulder. And flounder our way through the unfamiliar sounds of the Mourner's Kaddish. In unison. A duet for the dead. Uniting me with my brother. And with my tribe. Across the world. And across the centuries.

In this moment, I feel healed.

FINDING MY FAMILY

All my life, I have lived with many unanswered questions about my mother's family. I know they came from Lithuania. Apart from my grandparents who fled to South Africa to escape antisemitism, I didn't know their names. I didn't know where in Lithuania they lived. I knew a little about their death at the hands of the Russians and Germans, but I didn't know anything about their lives.

This was the purpose of my pilgrimage to Vilnius. To find answers.

I'd travelled with some of my soccer teammates to Russia to watch the 2018 Football World Cup. We were based in Kaliningrad, and I'd travelled to Vilnius, my family's homeland, during a four-day break between World Cup matches. My mates were happy to come along for the ride.

My mother knew very little of her family's life in Lithuania. Her parents, Reveka and Nisonas, rarely spoke of their past after they settled in South Africa. Mum told me that just once a year in the *Yizkor*, the prayer of remembrance for lost family members recited on holy days, they would pray for family they had lost. She told me of her childhood memories, seeing her father distraught on this day each year. The rest of the time, they focused on getting on with life. They had enough struggles each day. They didn't have the luxury of reflecting on the past.

I recall my mother telling me that her family was from Vilnius. Now I walked the streets of Vilnius, imagining I was treading in the

FINDING MY FAMILY

footsteps of my mother's ancestors. To walk where they may have once walked. To see and touch and smell what they once had.

I was in a trance, seeking out their spirits around every corner. All day, down every lane, in front of every building, like a snake whose tongue can taste vibrations in the air, I opened to the possibilities of my family's story.

And I found answers. I learnt that what I thought I knew of my family legend was not completely correct. And I learnt many new things too.

I visited the Jewish Centre of Culture and Information and spent hours with the woman who works there, trawling through databases searching for more information about my family. The only accurate information I had to offer her were my grandmother Reveka's date of birth, that her maiden name was something like Lurie, and that my grandfather's original family name may have been Busmanas.

We found nothing in the databases of births and deaths and passport applications. Finally, we looked at the marriage listings. We scrolled, quickly now, through hundreds of names, losing hope, when my eyes caught sight of this:

Lithuania Marriages and Divorces

Marriage Place Town / Uyezd / Guberniya	Groom Name	Groom Father Mother Place	Groom Age
Marriage Date (DD/MM/CCYY) HebrewDate	Bride Name	BrideFather Mother Place	Bride Age
Kursenai Siauliai Kaunas	BUSMANAS / [BUSMAN], Nisonas	Jankelis Leibas Seina Rive Vegeriai, Mazeikiai dist.	1906
23/6/1929	LURIJITE / [LURIE], Reveka	Ber Hirsas Hane Kursenai, Siauliai dist.	1901

'Stop!' I cried as I pointed at the listing at the top of the screen. 'That's them! That's my grandparents! Stop!'

The woman stopped scrolling. She was pleasant, in an off-hand manner, and clearly immune to these sorts of discoveries. Her eyes told me that she was happy for me, but the way her body remained facing toward the computer screen said she was hoping I wasn't going to be one of those diaspora Jews who come here and break down when they find a trace of their long-lost family.

I'm not sure how I did it, maybe years of practice holding my emotions at bay while bearing witness to the suffering of my patients, but I managed to restrict my emotional display to a pre-tears reddening of the eyes.

'That's them,' I said again, unsure whether I was trying to convince myself or the impassive woman beside me.

And that's how I found my great-grandmother Hane. Her husband Ben Hiras. My grandmother Reveka. Her husband Nisonas. Their extended families.

A miracle.

I kept my emotions under control until I returned to the apartment and my Aussie football friends. One of them, Rollo, was particularly excited about my quest. 'How did you go?' he asked as I walked in after this momentous discovery.

'I found my family!' I could barely talk through the tears. 'I know my grandparents' actual names! And their parents' names. And when they were born. And where they lived. And when they were married.'

Australian male footballers are trained not to show emotion. It's a sign of weakness. But I couldn't keep these tears of joy and grief and relief inside any longer. The excitement on my friends' faces washed away my shame. They stopped short of offering me a hug, but they were happy for me. And wanted to know the whole story.

I am so happy to have found my family. They were not from Vilnius after all. A lid has been lifted from a box filled with treasure. I have new family legends to absorb. With new heroes. New homelands. Many questions were answered, but not all. I am ready for the journey ahead.

ON MY MOTHER'S SIDE

My mother's parents migrated from Lithuania to South Africa as newlyweds in 1929. Their extended families, who stayed behind in Lithuania, were all killed during WWII. I barely knew my grandparents, who stayed in South Africa when we migrated to Australia. My mother said they never spoke of their past. Only a few photos remain of their life in Lithuania and their early days in South Africa. I have used these photos as the source for writing the following speculative journal entries. I had no family stories to draw upon. The writing process has helped me fall in love with family members I never knew. This was especially true when I wrote in the voice of my great-grandmother, Hane Lurijite, whom I knew absolutely nothing about.

ONE CURIOUS DOCTOR

Nisonas – Vegeriai, Lithuania, 1928

Hilton's maternal grandfather, Nisonas Busmanas (top right), in his barbershop.

I could be the luckiest Jew in Vegeriai. I don't have to work outside in the heat in summer or cold in winter. I don't have to cart goods from one town to another like other Jews do. Or slaughter animals. Or use a saw and hammer all day. My hands are still as soft as a child's, not battered and bruised by physical labour. I don't have to wear the same grubby overalls every day. I get to wear nice clothes that my sisters make for me.

I work as barber. It's a nice job. I get to talk with people all day. Sometimes, people come into the shop just to make coffee and sit

and talk with the customers and me. This I like. There's not so much money from a barbershop, but money isn't everything. Good friends are more important than money. For me.

Sometimes people come, they need a haircut, but have no money. Like today, a mother came with her three girls and two boys. The big boy, he's not right in the head. He pulls out handfuls of hair when he has his mental attacks. He always needs a short haircut. The girls, they want to look nice, like all girls do. Today, the mother only had enough money for a shave for the crazy boy. But I want her and the other children to look good too. I cut the other children's hair for free. And the mother's. She'll pay me next time. Or bring me turnips or beetroot from her garden. Everyone is happy this way. It's the best way.

Nisonas – 1928

Nisonas Busmanas (left).

I've been dragged into uniform. Into the Lithuanian army. Taken from my home, my family. My brother Meieras was conscripted with me. This is good for me. But bad for our family. Only my two sisters are left to help our parents. It's already so hard for the family. Now it will be even harder.

ONE CURIOUS DOCTOR

There are four other boys from Vegeriai in our unit. From only twenty Jewish families in our town. Six of us together in the army is good for us. Bad for our families. There are no young men left to help with the business of scrounging an income. How will they get on without us?

Nisonas – 1928

Nisonas Busmanas (middle row, second from right).

Army life is difficult. They train us to kill. Of course, this is the job of a soldier. The Lithuanian boys, they don't need much training. They're already good enough at killing. Their eyes are crazy for blood. For me, it's not so easy to learn to kill. I've killed a cow once and chickens a few times. So we can eat. But to kill a person, even a Polack or Russian, maybe I can't do that. I pretend. What else can I do? Maybe they'll kill me if I don't do what they say. Lithuanians, they love to kill Jew boys.

ON MY MOTHER'S SIDE

Nisonas – 1928

Nisonas Busmanas (centre, looking to his left).

Yesterday, Meieras and me and the other Vegeriai boys visited Kurseniai, a small town near Siauliai. We found a café. The coffee was sweet. Sweet coffee makes our stale cigarettes taste nearly good. All we can get on the black market is Russian smokes. Terrible, but better than nothing. It's good to have break. We train so hard. Orelis, he's asleep at the table. He's been visiting the prostitutes in town again. He never learns.

The woman who runs the café was friendly to us. For a Lithuanian. She's happy the army is trying to keep Lithuania safe from the Poles and Russians. She told us stories about how bad the Polacks and Russkies treated her.

She said the Jewish boys are the best behaved. That we're welcome anytime. 'Come back tomorrow, I'll introduce you to some Kursenai Jewish girls. Good girls. You boys will like them.'

So today I went back to the café with Meieras. Orelis and the other boys are too crazy for meeting nice girls. The boss lady introduced us. I like Reveka. She's pretty. And smart. She saw me writing a postcard

to my family in Vegeriai. She said that it's okay to write to her too and gave me her address. This made me happy. Happier than I've been for a long time. Maybe something good might come from this terrible time in the army. Maybe yes. Maybe no. Who can tell these days?

Hane Lurijite – 1929

Wedding of Reveka Lurijite to Nisonas Busmanas, Kursenai, Lithuania, 23 June 1929. Hane Lurijite, Hilton's maternal grandmother's mother, is seated far left.

Last month, we married off our middle daughter Reveka to Nisonas Busmanas. Today, the wedding photo arrived. It's my first time in a photo, a photo that brings back sadness from Reveka's wedding day. And so many questions.

A wedding is supposed to be day of joy, a *bentshung*, isn't it? If a blessing, why then is there no joy in our eyes? The photographer told us not to smile. Because that's the way for a photo. But we look like we're at a funeral. I think this is because we know what we are about to lose. How will we manage without Reveka? After she is gone, who will take her load? Already life is difficult enough.

ON MY MOTHER'S SIDE

Why did they sit me on that hard bench for the photo? My feet, they cannot even touch the floor. My shoes are ugly. Dangling like last year's garlic. Proof of our poverty. Compared to his family. Their pearls. So long. And the sister's dress. So short. At a wedding! I've never seen such a thing.

My husband Ber Hirsas, he sits with his eyes half closed. He thinks that if he does not look, then it will not happen. I am not surprised. All our marriage, he has been doing this. Me, I need to keep my eyes wide open. The wife, she is the one who must think about the future.

Nisonas' mother Siena looks like she has mental problems. Her mouth, the way it hangs down, it says she is never happy. A kiss from those lips could be dangerous. I pray that Nisonas has not been touched by the melancholy. And his father Jankelis, such crazy eyes bursting from his face, like he is sitting on a splinter. I think Nisonas has his father's eyes. Not his mother's mouth. That is better. It is easy to take a splinter out. But there is no cure for the melancholy.

What does my oldest daughter think about her younger sister being married first? And his parents, what do they think about Nisonas marrying a girl who is five years older than he is?

I cannot understand why Rabbi Jasguras allowed such a marriage. Our old ways of doing things, they are gone. The wars against the Russians and the Poles, they have given us freedom. But for what? For our traditions to be destroyed.

Why can't Reveka and Nisonas stay with us in our *shtetl* here in Kursenai? My family has lived here forever. Now the war is over, it is a good time to settle. To be with family. To make a family.

Why do they have to go so far away? How will they manage in South Africa? Reveka will have no family. No friends. They speak only Yiddish and some Lithuanian. Nisonas says we do not need to worry, there are plenty of Jews from Kursenai and other Lithuanian towns in South Africa. He says they will not be alone. But it is a mother's job to worry. What else can I do?

Last month, I dreamt that Reveka's spirit was taken by the *Dybbuk*. Such a nightmare on the eve of her wedding!

I pray that Nisonas takes good care of my girl. I pray they survive their journey to South Africa. That their new world treats them better than this place has treated us. That they make a family. And their family makes a family. That they overcome evil. The wars. The *Dybbuk*.

Then my family's spirits will have survived. And our suffering will have been for a good reason. This thought brings me joy. Maybe the wedding is a *bentshung* after all.

Reveka – Travelling from Lithuania to South Africa, 1929

Reveka and Nisonas Busmanas, Hilton's maternal grandparents.

Never have I imagined an ocean can be so big. Before getting on board the *Utena*, the only time I saw the sea was after our wedding when we went to Klaipeda for a few days. Seeing the sun setting over

the ocean there was like a miracle, a good omen for our married life together. Out here in the middle of the Atlantic Ocean, every day we can see the sun rise and set over the ocean. And the moon! And the stars. Never have I seen a night sky like this, when Nisonas and I walk on the upper deck after dinner.

Not that I have been eating much. I've been too sick. They said the sea sickness should only last a few days, but we've been gone over a week now and still I spend much of the time with my head in the bucket. It's strange, the seas are calm and no one else is sick. I pray there is no other reason. Now would not be the right time.

Married life has been good to me. With Nisonas' army pension, for the first time in my life, I was able to buy decent clothes. Some jewellery. I knew that Mame didn't approve. 'Why for you need to be spending so much on stupid fancy things? You can't eat fur or pearls', my mother would have been thinking. For once, it's nice to feel special. Nisonas said that after everything he saw in the army, it gives him joy to spend some of his pension money on me in this way. The rest we spent on getting to South Africa.

We had such a short time living with my family in Kursenai before we left. Saying goodbye, that was the most difficult thing. Poor Mame, she was heartbroken. She wouldn't come to see us off at the station for the train to Riga where we were to board the ship. I think she would have fainted as the train left the station. I feel so bad for doing this to her. But Nisonas was determined to leave Lithuania. He said the Jews would not survive another war. The Lithuanians tolerated us, but he saw from serving with them in the army how they could turn. He knew their enthusiasm for the kill. He said that for sure we were going to be their next target.

We pleaded with my family and his to come with us. They wouldn't leave. I wonder if I will ever see them again. I have to believe that Nisonas is my Moses, parting the seas to bring us to a Promised Land. The grief is too much to cope with otherwise.

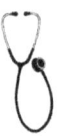

Rebecca (Reveka) – Bloemfontein, South Africa, 1935

Rebecca Baumann (Reveka Busmanas) with baby Ria (Hilton's mother) and David.

I never realised having two children would be so much more difficult than one. David's good, but he wants to be active, like a normal five-year-old. It's not so easy for me to be with David in the way I used to now that I have Ria to care for too.

All the Afrikaners and the English South Africans, they have maids to help them with their children. I can't do that. I could never trust the care of Ria or David to a native girl. Not with my heart, and not with my head. It's not the right thing to do. Mame Hane, if she were here, would never allow such a thing. Back in Kursenai, all the family helped with raising the kids – aunts, older sisters, grandparents. It's different for us here without family. But we manage.

Sometimes, I take Ria's highchair out into the back lane. She can sit there while David rides his bike. I see the light return to his face as he makes believe that he's got me all to himself, even for just a few

minutes. I wonder if it was like that for my older sister when I was born. I wish she were here for me to ask.

As much as I miss my parents and sisters and the rest of my family back home, my children are now my light. I never imagined I would feel such love. Especially after that terrible goodbye to my family. I thought if I put a shield of armour around my heart, and didn't let myself feel deeply again, then I'd be safe from the hurt of separation. But love was lying in wait, first for David, the year we arrived here, and now Ria.

I dream that my old family might come to meet my new family. I doubt that this will ever happen. Life must be getting more difficult for them. How can it be otherwise, with Russians on one side, Poles on the other, and that menace Germany getting uglier every day? Why can't they just leave my people to live in peace? For once.

Nathan (Nisonas) – 1945

Nathan Baumann (Nisonas Busmanas) at his store in a native township, Bloemfontein.

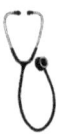

To feed four mouths is not so easy. This business barely supports us. Rebecca manages our finances with a firm hand, but there is only so much for her to share around. I want her to get a maid to help round the house, but she says, 'No, it's not our way. How can I trust to have a black girl in our home? And we can't afford it.'

I keep reminding myself why we made the journey to South Africa. To give us a chance at a life of freedom. But what freedom do we have? I'm here in this pathetic little shop for six days a week. The natives who come to buy things, they have less money than us. I think it is harder here than it was for my poor *tate*. At least as a peddler in Vegeriai my father knew all the customers. Sometimes he would sell on credit because he knew he would be paid. Eventually.

Here, it is so different. The natives, I can't understand their Zulu language. My English is too bad for them to understand. Afrikaans is a mystery. So they point at what they want and I hold up my fingers to say how much it costs. We get by, but it's no pleasure.

In winter, it's cold in the shop. In summer, too hot. I never knew such heat like here in Africa. It takes me nearly an hour to walk to the shop on the edge of the native township. Walking is no joy in summer, or when it rains. At least there is no snow. I don't like to get the bus to the shop. The bus is always full of blacks returning home after working all night in the factories in the city. They're made to crowd in the back of the bus while I have a choice of seats at the front. It's not right, but who am I to say anything. Being a troublesome Jew, it never ends well. I'd rather walk than have to keep my eyes on the floor of the bus, pretending that I don't see how bad it is for those up the back.

ON MY MOTHER'S SIDE

Nathan standing outside his home next to his friend Pincus' car.

Sometimes my friend Pincus will drive me. He's a good man, Pincus. We were in the army together. Once, back when we were on leave from the army, I helped him when he got arrested for being drunk. I got him out of a difficult situation. I think he still believes that he owes me, but when you're in the army, you look after your comrades. It's just what you do.

Pincus is lucky to have a job with the Chevra Kadisha, helping the undertakers clear out the dead person's house. And this is how he helps me too. He takes me to the house and lets me keep whatever I think might sell in my shop. Blankets. Jackets. Bags. Belts. Sometimes family treasures from the old country like platters or candlesticks. Seeing these things and knowing how far they've travelled, it makes me feel homesick. But who can afford to think about the past? Memories and tears don't feed my family. I offer to pay for the items I keep, but Pincus says, 'No need to pay. The families should be paying us for taking away their junk.' Pincus, he's made for business. Me, I'm not like that.

Sometimes we go to Pincus' house after the Friday evening synagogue service for Shabbat dinner. His wife Riva is a great cook. It's the best meal we eat for the whole month. They're kind to us. They tell us that if we ever need anything, just to ask. But I don't like to ask for charity. It's not how I was brought up.

I dream that one day I can start a barbershop again. I'm more suited to that work. With people I can talk to. I miss my old shop in Vegeriai. I wonder who is cutting hair for people there now. Maybe no one is having haircuts. Maybe everyone is just trying to stay safe from the troubles of the war. I need to stop complaining. It's not so bad here after all.

Nathan (Nisonas) – 1948

Nathan Baumann, Bloemfontein.

ON MY MOTHER'S SIDE

I'm finally getting used to Bloemfontein, feeling like I fit in. My hometown of Vegeriai only had a few hundred people. I knew everyone. Kursenai, where we lived with Rebecca's family for a short time after we were married, was bigger, but, still, all the Jews knew each other. They were a close community. Rebecca still misses that very much. She doesn't have the same chances like me to get out of the house. I need to encourage her to do that more.

On Sundays, when my store is closed, I put on my suit and formal hat, and catch the bus into the city to meet with other Lithuanians for a coffee. It reminds me of when I was a barber back home. I always liked to dress in the suits my sisters made for me. My friends would visit me in the shop and we'd share a coffee. Nearly every day I had such company.

Here, it's different. The Lithuanian Jews I know are spread over town. It's only a small city, but big enough that we're too far apart to meet during the week. So we make time to meet on a Sunday. Just the boys. It's different from when we see each other at *Shul* on a Friday night or Saturday morning. At the synagogue, we have our families with us. We can't talk openly. It's good to be with the families, but I like it when it's just the boys. We can say what we think.

I don't tell Rebecca what we talk about in the café. And she doesn't ask. I think she knows that it's a time for us to talk about our past. About what we've lost. I don't want to talk about those things in front of the women or children. It wouldn't be right. So at home, Rebecca and I focus on the present and think just a little about the future. The past is past. We don't need to discuss it anymore. This pact of silence, it suits us both well.

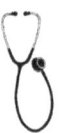

Rebecca (Reveka) – 1959

Nathan and Rebecca Baumann with Hilton, Johannesburg.

It's taken thirty years, but finally Mame Hane's wish for us has come true. After we left Lithuania for South Africa, she sent just one letter. I wonder who wrote it for her. Maybe Nikolai at the post office. He was always good to our family. I wonder if she knew it would be her only letter to us. Before the Lithuanian collaborators finished her off along with the rest of my family.

Mame sent the photo from our wedding. Such a gift. It's the only photo we have of our family together. She made me laugh the way she described her embarrassment at the shabbiness of her clothes compared to Nathan's family and about the bench being too high for her feet to touch the ground. I wish she could see us now. Making the train journey from Bloemfontein to Johannesburg to meet my grandson for the first time gives me an excuse to wear my best outfit, but my legs, they're also too short for my feet to touch the ground. Looks like I've inherited more than just

ON MY MOTHER'S SIDE

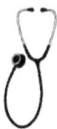

Mame's ability to see the funny side of life's awkward moments.

Nathan doesn't know whether to smile or cry. I know that look. He's working hard to keep the tears away. He knows that once the dam breaks open, even with tears of joy, the floodgates are hard to close again. He doesn't want to spoil this precious moment.

And neither do I. But I'm finding it hard to believe that after everything we have been through, everything we have lost, we finally have a grandchild. It's like God has shone a beam of radiance into our laps.

I'm doing my best to focus on the joy of becoming a grandmother, but this light that emanates from Hilton, it brings into sharper focus the shadows that lurk behind. It feels in some strange way that Mame is here with me, her gentle reassuring hand on my left shoulder, and yet I know she's so horribly absent.

I need to remember to look in front, not behind. That's what Nathan is always telling me. This time, I think he might be right.

Rebecca (Reveka) – 1995

Rebecca Baumann, Bloemfontein.

ONE CURIOUS DOCTOR

I have seen so much in my life. Too much. Now, it's hard to see anything. Even with these spectacles like magnifying glasses. What a blessing. I find the blur a relief. I don't need to see details now. Shapes and shadows are enough.

When they did the cataract operation years ago, they offered to put new lenses into my eyes. They said I would be able to see things sharp and clear again. Why would an old woman want that? Now, when I've had enough, I take my glasses off and I am at peace with the hazy world around me.

One of the kind nurses here read me a poem the other day. I didn't understand most of it, but I think it was about a famous artist who also had cataracts. They had offered him an operation to fix his vision, but he didn't want it. I asked her to repeat one of the lines that reminded me of how I felt. I think it went something like this: *Doctor, you say that what I see is a problem caused by old age, but I tell you that it has taken me all my life to arrive at the vision of streetlamps as angels.* (Adapted from 'Monet Refuses the Operation' by Lisel Meuller.)

Why would I let them take these angels from me?

Rebecca and Ray (Hilton's mother), Bloemfontein, 1995.

ON MY MOTHER'S SIDE

My Ray came yesterday. She's visiting from Australia. It's been too long since we were together. She sat with me for a few hours. Such precious time. Ray rested her soft hand gently on mine. Not being able to see allows the other senses to flourish. The love that radiated from her touch remains imprinted across the back of my weathered hands. Hands that I might not recognise even if I could see them. In this quiet moment, the connection flooded back. The magic that flows between mother and daughter. Like it was never interrupted by the ocean that separated us.

ON MY FATHER'S SIDE

When my father Bert died in 2013, the Koppe family albums came into my care. I have used these photos to tell the story of my father's parents, Rosi Kanin and Kurt Koppe. What follows are excerpts from imagined journals that Rosi and Kurt may have written during their lives. Some of the stories are based on recollections of family tales. Others are pure speculation conjured from details in the photos.

ON MY FATHER'S SIDE

Kurt – Hamburg, 1907

Kurt Koppe, standing, with his brother Manfred.

Manfred and I love to get out of Hamburg to go hiking. Hiking with Manfred is not easy because of his epilepsy. We need to take it slow. I don't mind. Sometimes I see more this way, when we take our time and sit for a while so Manfred can recover.

Manfred says that each person has only so many heartbeats allotted to them for their life. 'Why use all your heart beats in a rush?' I'd probably be lost without Manfred.

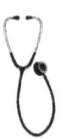

ONE CURIOUS DOCTOR

Kurt – Hamburg, 1916

Koppe Brothers building, Hamburg (from a newspaper advertisement).
Sign on roof: 'Our factory workshops'
Sign second floor: 'Fine men's clothing tailoring'
Ground floor sign (L): 'Professional laundry. Koppe Brothers. Men's clothing'
Ground floor sign (R): 'Men's clothing made to measure'

All my life, I've wanted to be a doctor. I've had to wait for my time to study. First, my older brother Manfred needed to study. He was very clever and became a doctor of law. During this time, I worked in our family business, Gebruder Koppe, to help my father. My father started the business after Manfred and I were born. He wanted us to have jobs when we finished school. It's easier for us Jews if we own a business.

ON MY FATHER'S SIDE

Kurt – 1916

Kurt Koppe (far right) standing in a trench.

Our glorious Kaiser and his army chief of staff, Helmuth von Moltke, have introduced conscription to provide fodder for the blood-thirsty generals and their stupid war. Just when Manfred finished his studies and it was my turn, I've been forced into the army, along with any other men fit enough to bear arms.

We've been given intense training before they send us to the Eastern front. Last week it was marching all day long. Sometimes overnight. I let my mind wander with each step, allowing my dreams to transport me somewhere different. A different time. A better place. When I was with Manfred, rambling together on the trails of Mellenberg or Tafelberg or Kaiserstuhl during our summer vacations.

This week, it's trench digging. For me, this is terrible. I'm not right for this sort of life. The Prussians and the Bavarians, they're big men. With broad shoulders to match their moustaches. They can dig. Their hands are already calloused from their work in the mines or the railways. All I've ever handled is a pen, not a pickaxe.

Kurt – 1916

Kurt Koppe (middle row standing, seventh from left).

Our rudimentary training is over and we've been shipped like cattle south-east to Osijek. We've just finished our first month of active duty.

Life in the trenches, it's terrible. After only a month, even the Bavarians don't look so tough anymore. Dysentery has taken hold. Randolf, who is sitting in front of me, can barely stay upright. He needs medical care, but there's no such thing here.

ON MY FATHER'S SIDE

Kurt – 1916

Kurt Koppe (middle row, second from right) at the German Servicemen's Hospital.

I got sick soon after our last deployment. The diarrhoea, it didn't stop. You don't want to imagine in the trenches how bad that was. I lost weight. Got so weak, I thought I might die. Our army was doing well, so they could afford to spare a Jewish weakling. I got evacuated to the field hospital and then onto this repatriation hospital. I think the Prussians and the Bavarians were happy to see me go. I was never much use to them.

I fit in better here. There are fewer bear-like man-monsters. Some of the other patients even like to read. We're treated as equals. Whether you've lost a leg, or have facial burns, or just intractable diarrhoea, the nurses care for us all with kindness and compassion. They're angels, the nurses. I never imagined that my life would lead me to a place where I'd need to put myself in the hands of Catholic nuns. Mother would be horrified.

They're under orders to do their best to fatten me up with soups and potatoes so they can send me back to the front line. But my guts,

they're ruined. I don't think I'll be good for anything after this. If I stay this skinny, surely they can't send me out again, especially with winter coming. I'd never survive.

Kurt – 20 March 1923

Kurt with older brother Manfred, Hamburg, 1894.

After the war, after everything I've seen, 20 March 1923 is the saddest day of my life. My brother, my best friend, Manfred, dead. Barely thirty-two years old. From the time I was a baby, we were very close. I felt nothing but *gemütlichkeit*, such warmth and good cheer, when I was with him.

Last night, he went out with his friends. Maybe he had too much to drink and when he came home, he forgot to take his medicine. He must have had a terrible seizure in the night. No one knew. No one heard. He died alone.

ON MY FATHER'S SIDE

I found him this morning when I went to his room to call him for breakfast. Lying soiled in his excrement. Tongue chewed through worse than a Rottweiler with a rag doll. His skin a patchwork of mottled purple. I'm no stranger to death, but he looked the deadest of anyone I've ever seen. Is that even possible? My poor Manfred. What a terrible way to die.

I regret now my petty jealousy that he got to study while I worked in the family business. Why did I waste so much effort complaining about how my time in the trenches ruined my health? Manfred never complained. I wish I could be more like him.

Rosi – 1925

Rosi Kanin.

I love to sit at my desk, strewn with books and my wildly speculative poems, my mind's eye focused on a future beyond what I know.

Mamma encourages me to pursue my love of technical drawing even though I am the only girl in the class. And she encourages me to write poetry. She tells me that she wants me to have a rich and varied life. 'You must be yourself, Rosi. You don't have to succumb to the constraints of past traditions.' I am blessed to be growing up in such an environment. To be entering adulthood during our enlightened modern times.

Rosi Kanin (centre), with friends, Hamburg.

On summer weekends, I take the tram with my friends to the hills outside of Hamburg for picnics. Mamma doesn't worry that boys and girls are picnicking together. She trusts me. I don't think she has told Papa what I am doing on these forays to the countryside. I am not sure he would be quite as agreeable.

ON MY FATHER'S SIDE

Rosi – 1927

Rosi with Uncle Nathan Kanin, Hamburg.

Last week, my father's brother, Dr Nathan Kanin, visited us at our new Hamburg home. He lives in South Africa. He loves to tell stories.

'After I graduated from medical school in Leipzig,' he said, 'I joined the Dutch Navy as a ship's doctor. My first mission was to Durban. When we docked, I heard that the only European doctor in South Africa had died. So I jumped ship and rode on horseback to Johannesburg to take up his position.

'During the Boer War, I served with the Boers but as the British came into ascendency, I jumped ship again and took charge of the British military hospital. Lord Kitchener even sent me a personal letter of thanks.'

He also told a wild tale about picnicking with Stanley, of 'Dr Livingstone, I presume' fame, and that the event was such a big deal that it was even reported in the local newspaper.

ONE CURIOUS DOCTOR

I am not sure I could believe all his stories. How could one man have so many adventures?

Nathan Kanin, South Africa.

I was charmed and enchanted by his life. His world is like something from the wild west of America. He seems so alive. I have never met anyone like him. Surely there are important things that I can learn from this tall dark mysterious uncle, so different to my own father!

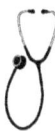

ON MY FATHER'S SIDE

Ludwig Kanin, Rosi's father.

During his visit to Hamburg, Uncle Nathan was invited to give a public lecture about venereal disease. Uncle Nathan is a leading specialist in this field. He believes that the way to avoid the problems of venereal disease is to prevent people from getting the infection. Unlike most of the medical profession, he is not puritanical about it. He is realistic. He wants to promote the correct use of condoms as a way of preventing venereal disease.

I went to his public lecture. The lecture hall was full of young people. We had to push our way through the crowds of protesters out the front. The police did little to protect us. As I neared the entrance, I was pushed against a man to my right. He caught me before I fell. Quite a strange way to meet a man!

As it turned out, we had met before. He reminded me of his name, Kurt Koppe, and that he had escorted my sister Else to the Textile Industry Ball a few weeks earlier.

ONE CURIOUS DOCTOR

After the lecture, Kurt offered to walk me home. We stopped for a coffee on the way. He told me a little about his time in the army. He had suffered greatly from the terrible conditions. I found the determination in his manner appealing. Yet he has sadness in his eyes. We are going to meet again next week. I'm excited about life's possibilities.

Kurt – 1927

Rosi Kanin and Kurt Koppe.

Today I met with Rosi Kanin as we'd arranged last week. I arrived at her home thirty minutes early. A gentleman must always be punctual, but even by my usual cautious approach to life, this was completely *mshuge*.

I suggested that we take the tram to Hasselbrack Hill. We walked and talked and shared afternoon coffee. Rosi listened to my stories about my time in the army with care and compassion. I ended up saying more than I had expected. It was cold outside and there had been an unusually heavy snowfall, but I felt a wondrous warmth being close to Rosi.

ON MY FATHER'S SIDE

She told me about growing up in Manheim. About her gentle, kind mother. Her stern father. The opposite of my family! She is very close to her two sisters. Like I had been with Manfred.

I've always believed that it's important for a woman to come from a good family, and this certainly seems to be the case with Rosi. A man must be cautious in affairs of the heart. The head must rule the heart. I'm so glad that my head continues to confidently nod its approval.

I summonsed up the courage to ask Rosi if we could exchange photographs. I've read that this is the right thing to do at the start of a romance. Even though I'm thirteen years older than her, I want her to know that I'm a modern man. I was delighted when she agreed.

Kurt – 1927

Kurt Koppe, 1916 and 1927

I spent a lot of time trying to choose the best photo to send to Rosi. In the end, I couldn't decide between two, so I sent them both. One is from my early army days, before the dysentery got hold of me. I hope that being in uniform portrays me as the resilient man Rosi might be looking for. The other photo was a closer portrait. I like the play of light and shadow on my face, a metaphor for my past and my future. Rosi likes poetry. I trust that she will see the symbolism embedded in the images.

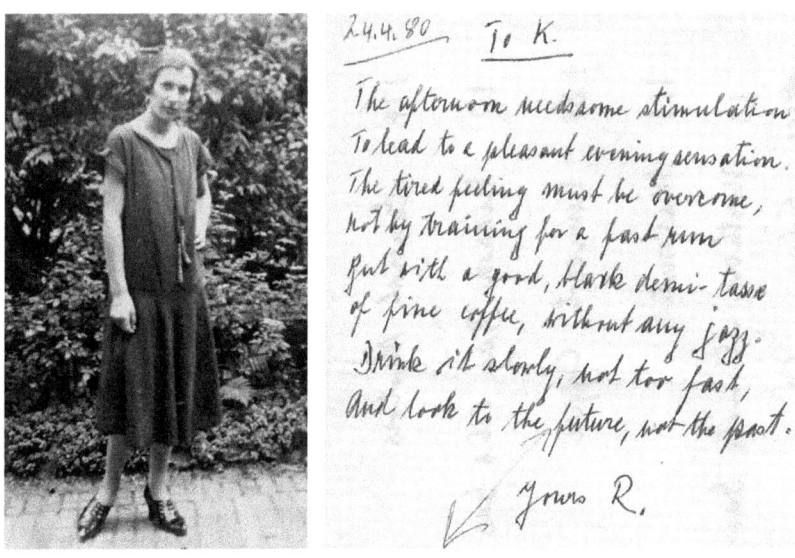

Rosi Kanin, Hamburg, 1925;
Poem from Rosi to Kurt (written in 1980, appropriated).

Today, a letter arrived in the morning mail for me. What a gift. The most beautiful photo of Rosi, a halo of light above her. The photo was accompanied by a poem.

> *To K.*
>
> *The afternoon needs some stimulation*
> *To lead to pleasant warming sensation.*
> *The tired feeling must be overcome,*
> *Not by training for a fast run*
> *But with a good, black demi-tasse*

ON MY FATHER'S SIDE

Of fine coffee, without any jazz.
Drink it slowly, not too fast,
And look to the future, not the past.
Yours R

She understands me! Like no one else ever has. My breath, it has been stolen.

Rosi – March 1930

Wedding of Rosi Kanin to Kurt Koppe.

Today I became Frau Koppe. We had a simple marriage lunch at my parent's home. Kurt and I did not want a synagogue wedding. Money is short, so lunch at our home was perfect. It is the happiest day of my life. Kurt was sad that his brother had not survived to see us married. I have learnt to let him have these blue moments, and then gently focus his attention back to the future. On this brightest of bright spring days, our future did indeed glow with possibilities.

Rosi – 1933

Kurt, with Bert and Stephan, Hamburg, September 1933.

On 7 October last year, two days after my twenty-fifth birthday, Stephan Harald was born. Now Bert has a little brother. Stephan is a completely different boy, full of smiles and on the go right from the start. How can two boys from the one set of parents be so different?

Kurt is uncertain as a father. Always so formal. His mother had been the dominant parent in his family, so maybe he's not sure what a father is supposed to do. My father was like that too. I wonder if this is normal for German men. Maybe when the boys get a little older he will be able to relax and become more involved with them. Boys need a father to look up to. Not someone to fear.

ON MY FATHER'S SIDE

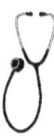

Rosi – Brussels, 1933

Rosi with Kurt, Bert and Stephan, Hamburg, September 1933.

Sitting with Kurt and our boys in the park near our apartment last Sunday, how was I to know that these may have been our final days in Hamburg?

One of Kurt's employees has been trying to bribe him. He threatened Kurt that if he didn't hand over the equivalent of six months wages, he would tell the Brownshirts that Kurt had been drumming up opposition to Hitler. Kurt refused to pay and immediately sacked him. Yesterday, a group of Brownshirts entered Kurt's business and took him away.

I was home when one of our employees came to tell me what had happened. I went straight to the police station. Kurt was being held by a group of young men with an arrogance that comes from unhindered power. I noticed a quieter boy towards the back of the group. It was

Hans, the son of our neighbour. I had known Hans since he was a baby. This was our chance.

'Hans,' I said, looking straight at him. 'We helped your family during the Depression. When things were difficult for them. Now things are difficult for us. It's your turn to help us. Please, Hans. Let Kurt go.'

Hans was the senior Brownshirt on duty. Ridiculous that a mere child could oversee another family's future. But miraculous for us. The thugs looked to him for guidance. 'Okay, Frau Koppe. You and Herr Koppe may leave. But you must leave Hamburg. Today. If the boys catch you again, I won't be able to intervene. Now go. Both of you. Go – and don't come back.'

As we rode the tram back to our apartment, we made a list of what to take with us. Kurt's mother came as we packed. Kurt gave her instructions on how to manage the business. There was no time to say goodbye to other family members. Just time to gather some cash and pack the essentials.

We caught the 7 pm train from Hamburg to Brussels. Once we stepped onboard, I feared that we would not see Hamburg again. As for our families, I had no idea what might happen to them.

This morning, through the train's grimy windows, I witnessed the sun coming up over Belgian fields. How quickly life can change. And yet, somehow, in some strange way, I feel that we may be the lucky ones.

ON MY FATHER'S SIDE

Rosi – 1935

Rosi with Bert and Stephan, Paris, 1935.

At last, I feel like I can breathe again. We've been on the move for three months. First it was Brussels. A distant cousin took us in for a time, but the Belgian government wouldn't let us stay. It was the same in Holland. Governments are scared of accepting fleeing Jews.

France has been more welcoming. My fluency in French helps. We've found an apartment in a nice neighbourhood of Paris. Kurt's works emptying cigarette machines in cafés. The Parisians smoke so much, he'll never be out of a job. He's improving his rudimentary French by sharing a coffee with the locals at each café on his rounds. He seems happier than I have seen him in years.

Bert, Paris, 1935.

Our apartment is small, but the parks in Paris, they are extraordinary. We've managed to save a little money and bought a bike for Bert. It's a joy to see him happy again.

It feels like we are leading a normal life again. I hope that it lasts.

ON MY FATHER'S SIDE

Rosi – 1936

Rosi Koppe, aboard TSS Canterbury, *sailing from France to England.*

Despite the optimism that we shared with our families at our wedding table a few years ago, here we are, after the most difficult of times, taking a boat across the English Channel, on our way to begin a new life in South Africa without them. Our life in Paris was good. The boys were happy. Kurt enjoyed his job. I felt at ease with the French. But Kurt was becoming increasingly anxious about Germany. He suggested that I contact my Uncle Nathan. I had often spoken to Kurt about his visit to my family when I was younger and of the freedom of his life in South Africa. Kurt yearned for such freedom. A new country. A fresh start.

Uncle Nathan was exceptional. He arranged for us to travel to South Africa. Visas. Boat tickets. Money. He did everything. Is it possible that a man can also be an angel? That's how Uncle Nathan has been for us.

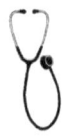

ONE CURIOUS DOCTOR

Kurt – England, 1936

Kurt Koppe's Certificate of Registration as an Alien, England, 23 November 1936.

And now, upon entry to England to transit to South Africa, I'm classified as an alien. No better than a creature from outer space.

Rosi – December 1936

Stephan, Bert and Kurt, aboard Stirling Castle *sailing to South Africa, 1936.*

For the last three years, our small family has been on the move. We have no choice. We need to be safe. We have two little boys. What else is a mother to do? And so, our family journey continues. Once again, we need to pack our things. Take what we can fit in a few battered old suitcases. Our jewellery hidden in coat linings. Kurt says it's better not to attract attention. No wedding rings. No necklaces. Just simple clothing. The safe way. The way Jews have travelled for centuries. The rest of what we have been able to keep through all the moves will come by cargo. These few belongings are the only connections to home. I pray that it all arrives safely in South Africa.

ONE CURIOUS DOCTOR

For once, Kurt is the confident one. He has seen from his time in the war what people are capable of. He wants us as far away as possible from that potential. The further we travel, the more relaxed Kurt becomes. He even ventures on deck without a tie. He is a changed man.

I hope things will be okay for our boys. Stephan, he will be fine. Bert, it's harder to tell. He is trying so hard to be brave. To be happy. But I sense his heart was broken when we had to move again.

I am not a religious woman, but I have found myself praying for our future. What harm can it do?

Kurt – Turffontein Racecourse, Johannesburg, 1938

Kurt Koppe (left) with Dr Nathan Kanin.

ON MY FATHER'S SIDE

He might have saved our lives, but it's so hard spending time with Uncle Nathan. His cigarette smoke finds its way up my nose. Already, before the crazy horseracing mob arrives, he's had too much to drink. He leans in closer, explaining his strategies for successful betting like a rabbi expounding the virtues of Jewish mysticism in the *Kabbalah*. To be forever in his debt and repulsed by him at the same time, this is difficult for me.

It's one thing to enjoy horse riding. But the absurdity of betting on horse races. Such nonsense, a doctor like Uncle Nathan behaving like a fool. How do they say it in English? 'More money than good sense.' Maybe it should be 'More stupidity than dollars and cents'.

He is so different to Rosi's father. Ludwig is one of the most serious men I have met. He writes long lists highlighting the risks and benefits of making even minor purchases. What does Ludwig think of his brother gambling like a commoner?

But I need to pretend that I'm enjoying my big day at the races. 'Come and live a little, Kurt,' Uncle Nathan implored. 'It'll do you good. Get you away from your worries for an afternoon.'

I must remember that our lives would be very different if it wasn't for his generosity. If he hadn't been willing to spend a small fortune to get us out of Europe. So that I can have a big day at the races.

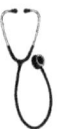

ONE CURIOUS DOCTOR

Rosi – date uncertain

Men are not immortal creatures, endorsed with hidden supernatural powers, but merely representatives of an intelligent animal species, evolving bravely on a small planet in a complex and possibly hostile universe. The idea of an afterlife is simply ceasing to be either meaningful or credible.

ON MY FATHER'S SIDE

Kurt – Manly, Sydney, 1986

Kurt Koppe in his flat at Manly.

I'm getting tired now. So tired. Since they put the pacemaker in my heart, it's hard to do much. I don't know why they did it. My heart was trying to give everyone the message that I have been saying for the last few years. I've had enough. I've seen enough. Some nights I just want to go to sleep and not wake up.

I love to sit in my rocking chair, rug on my lap, close my eyes and let my mind drift. The older I get, the more easily I can see the past.

Kurt with Bert, Hamburg, 1931.

Fatherhood wasn't easy for me. My mother was such a strong influence in my childhood, I wasn't sure how to be a good father. I think that maybe I was too stiff with the boys. More like a statue than a loving father.

Kurt and Rosi with baby Hilton, Johannesburg, 1959.

It was easier when the grandchildren came along. Rosi was by my side, as always, guiding me. 'Relax, Kurt,' she whispered. 'Rejoice in this moment with all your senses. It's such a blessing. Who would have thought, as we were on the run from the Nazis, that the day would come where you could hold a grandson in your arms?'

Kurt Koppe with Hilton (left) and Allen, Sydney.

As my grandsons grew and we settled into a peaceful life in Australia, I loved their visits to our flat here in Manly. I can still feel the heft of Hilton and Allen on my lap while I told them stories from my old world. I read them stories they didn't get at school. European stories. Struwwelpeter. The Brothers Grimm Fairy Tales. Stories that transported me from Manly to my childhood. I wonder what Hilton and Allen will remember of these times. Such happy times for me. Hopefully for them too.

Kurt with Hilton, St Ives, 1963.

ONE CURIOUS DOCTOR

The visits Rosi and I made to Bert's family home in St Ives were such a delight. Where I came from, no one could live in a city and have farms next door and trees across the road. It was the right decision to leave South Africa and come to Australia. And, of course, to leave Germany before that.

In my lifetime, I have seen so many changes. I think enough now.

Kurt with Rosi and Bert, Manly, 1986.

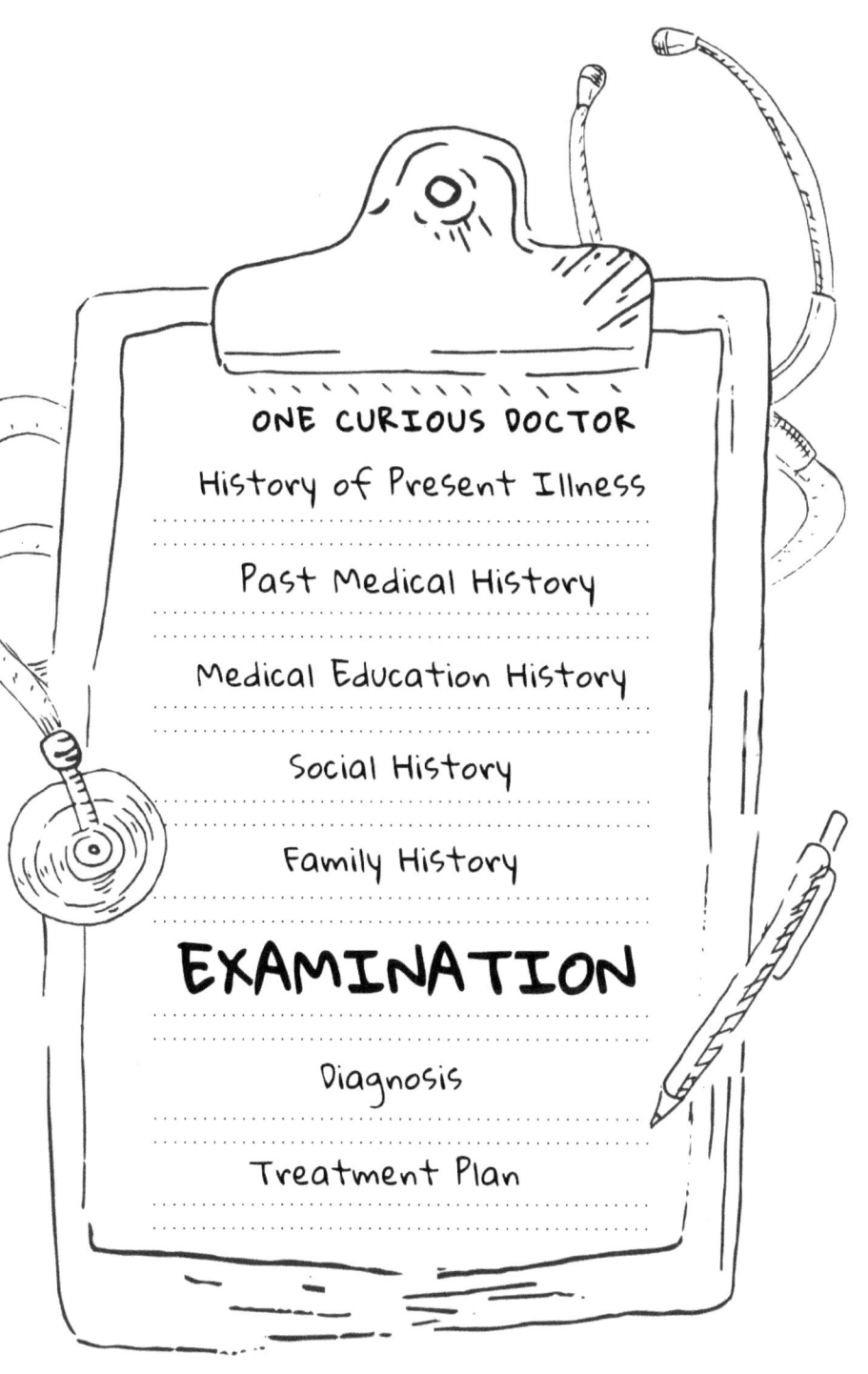

MATCH OF THE DAY

MICK: Greetings sports fans and welcome to the Weird World of Sports! Micky Kid here for today's battle brought to you live from the cauldron of nervous tension, The Hill Medical Centre. Joining me as usual in the commentary position is a doc who has done more than his fair share of home visits, the immortal who has dealt with more sick kids than a nanny goat, the man who has redefined what it means to be a GP, Professor Johnny Murto!

PROF: Thanks Mick, great to be here with you. I think we're about to see an epic struggle and the viewers at home are in for quite a treat.

MICK: I couldn't agree more Prof. Today we're going to see a fatiguing country doc up against one of the meanest, the sickest, and dare I say it, the most litigious lists of patients that any GP would have nightmares about.

PROF: You're right Mick. I've had a look at his list for today, and he's in for a shocker. Plus, he's coming back from a week at a conference, where no doubt he overindulged in pharmaceutical sponsored largesse. We all know about his reputation in this regard. I'm surprised we didn't see his name in the headlines again.

MICK: So how's he going to approach the battle today, Prof?

PROF: Well, if he's going to get through the day with his sanity intact and get home to see his kids before they go to bed, he is going to have to rely on all his experience and self-directed learning to get the upper hand early, take control of the visits and ensure that he runs to time. We've seen what happens once he gets behind, and he just can't afford to do that today.

MICK: I agree Prof. I'm not expecting to see too many open-ended questions. I think he'll go for more of an orthopaedic approach, if not right from the start, then definitely if he starts getting bogged down in emotionally leaden problems.

PROF: Yep, sure Mick, I wouldn't want to see an insecure personality disorder on the list today. It could be carnage.

MICK: Let's cross live now to the clinic room to see how the doc is preparing for the punishment of his first day back at the coalface. It's good to see that he's got in a bit earlier than usual, and that he was able to ride his bike instead of driving. The stats clearly show he does much better on days when he rides. Clears the head and helps with focus.

PROF: He's going to need all the clarity he can get today after all the claret he drank last week.

MICK: Luckily, it looks like his results have been checked by the other doctors while he was away, which will help him to get off to an on-time start. We'll keep a check on his fitness to practice during the session via our Holter Heart Tracker. But right now, he's had a quick scan of the patient list for today and is ready to open the first patient file. Who's coming in, Prof?

PROF: You wouldn't believe it Mick, but his first patient is a WorkCover case. It looks like the certificate runs out today, which will make the doc feel more confident about getting this patient out quickly. Oh no, look at the diagnosis on the certificate.

MATCH OF THE DAY

MICK: PTSD! What a way to start the week. Let's see how he handles this one. He's shepherded the patient from the crowded waiting room straight to his room, and is guiding the conversation directly to the certificate. But the patient has other ideas. He hasn't spent the last four weeks waiting for this appointment to be fobbed off with just a certificate. He wants to talk about not sleeping. And feeling tired! What a killer for the doc. A fatigued PTSDer!

PROF: But can you see how he's handling this. He's using the old 'We can't expect the insurance company to pay for non-work-related complaints' line. It's an oldie, but it's certainly very effective today.

MICK: I don't know if a younger doctor could have got away with that. The doc couldn't have asked for a smoother start to the day.

PROF: Yeah, Mick, the doc is clearly an expert at making his patients believe that he's giving them what they want and …

MICK: Prof, I've got to interrupt you there. Look what's happening. He's got one of his co-dependent patients in the consulting room. You'll remember her, she's followed him to three different practices and always has insoluble problems.

PROF: Let's check his Holter Heart Tracker! Just as I suspected, you can see that his heart is sinking. He's going to have to dig deep to get through this one without going into extra time.

MICK: I can't believe what I'm seeing Prof. He's actually showing the patient the timer on the computer medical record and reminding her that normal appointments are for 15 minutes only and they are up to 12 minutes already. I don't think I've ever seen a doctor do that on live TV. Surely he knows the cameras are on him. It's a very risky play.

PROF: But he's doing it so stylishly that I'm sure the patient doesn't realise it's a ploy to get her out. He's thrown her a dummy with the

line 'Out of respect to the other patients in the waiting room, we're going to have to wind things up for today'.

We're seeing a master in action here today, Micky. He's doing what we used to call …

MICK: Sorry to interrupt again, Prof, but there's a bit of a ruckus going on in the waiting room. Billy Snodgrass is here.

PROF: Ah Billy. The most hyperactive ADHD kid in the practice. I used to hate seeing kids like Billy. But our doc has a bit of a reputation at being good with these kids. Let's see how he handles this one.

MICK: The doc's arrived in the waiting room just as the box of blocks is being tipped upside down. See how Billy's mum hasn't sat down but is hovering behind Billy clearing up whatever mess he creates. What a great job she's doing. And the doc is acknowledging this with a glance in her direction as he greets Billy. But this is no normal doctor greeting. He's being even louder than Billy!

PROF: I think he's trying to appear to be at least as excited about life as Billy is. And it's working. Billy has stopped throwing blocks at his baby sister and seems interested in this noisy adult. What's this? The doc has offered to race Billy into his room! That's the most unheard-of thing I've ever heard of, Mick.

MICK: And now he's starting the visit with Billy sitting on the floor near the toy box in his room. I've never seen anything like this before.

PROF: This isn't in my book, Micky, but I'm going to put it in the next edition. What a masterstroke!

MICK: Oh, no! He's going to need to examine Billy, this could get ugly. He's asked Billy to lift his shirt …

PROF (yelling): He's down, Mick! The doc is down!

MATCH OF THE DAY

MICK: I didn't see what happened there, it must have been something in the back play. Let's see if our reverse angle super slow-mo camera can pick up what happened. Yes, there it is, as the doc reached over to lift Billy's shirt, he's copped him a nasty blow in the groin.

PROF: Argh, that's gotta hurt. We all love to see a tough physical exam, but that sort of blow is sickening.

MICK: Let's see what the officials do here. Yes, there it is, the practice manager has given Billy a straight red, off he goes for an early shower with his mum chasing behind him without even stopping to sign the Medicare voucher. Well, I don't know about you, Prof, but I'm exhausted from watching that. While the doc gets some much-needed attention from the practice nurse, it's time to return to the station for the latest news headlines. We'll be back after the weather with a wrap-up of the day's play here at the cauldron.

MICK: Welcome back, sports fans, for the final stages of today's battle. As we saw earlier in the broadcast, the doc got off to a brilliant start, but as the day has gone on, the patient load has worn him down. Amazingly, he was able to get back into his chair after that killer blow from Billy, but it clearly took its toll. How have you seen the day's play, Prof?

PROF: Well, I agree, Mick, that the doc hasn't been able to maintain the energy of his enthusiastic start. It can't have been easy for him out there. His colleague's away on representative duties and no locums on the bench.

MICK: Let's cross now live for some final views of the doc as he wraps things up. He's still got three prescriptions, a referral and an insurance medical report to complete. I can't see him getting past the

prescriptions tonight. Well, thanks for your company throughout the day, Prof.

PROF: It's been my pleasure, Mick. I can't wait for the clash in tonight's late game as we head over live to the Emergency Department to see how they handle all those patients who couldn't get appointments in general practice during the day.

MICK: And remember viewers, you can follow live updates on our Medicare-approved website, and we'll be back with a summary of all the week's action on the Morbidity and Mortality Show on Tuesday night. Till then, bye for now from all of us at the Weird World of Sports.

ODE TO MY STETHOSCOPE

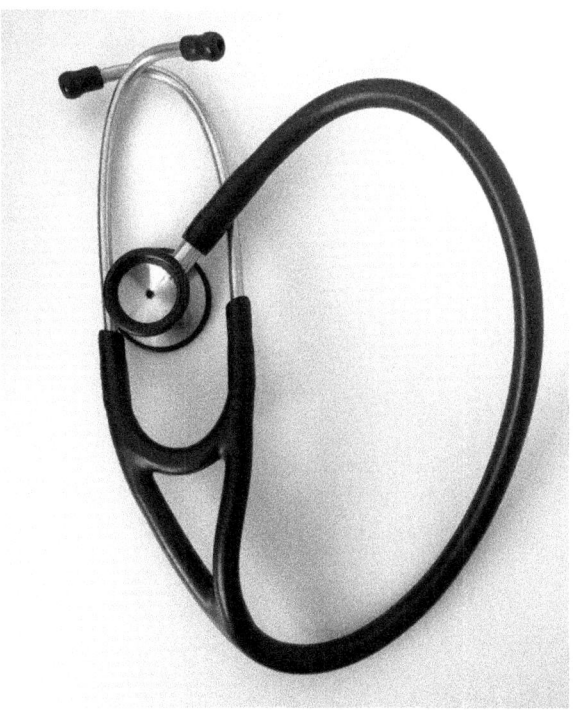

My Littman stethoscope has accompanied me on my journey in medicine across five decades and into premature medical retirement. It was definitely more difficult to lay down my stethoscope than it had been for me to recommend medical retirement to many of my patients. This poem includes a liberal sprinkling of medical terminology, which I hope has sufficient musical quality to sustain the poem's meaning, as well as mirroring the mystery of what a doctor hears when they listen to a patient's heart.

ONE CURIOUS DOCTOR

Ode to my stethoscope

What if I were to lay you down, my faithful companion? We have journeyed together across five decades, to medical schools on three continents, clinics in six states. You opened many hearts
to me. Helped me hear what is hidden to most. Subtle murmurs of the heart,
innocent and pathological. Shunts of congenital anomalies. Valves, porcine
and mechanical. Flutterings. Fibrillations. Skipped beats.
The slow rhythmic LUB DUB of the athlete.
LUB shhhh DUB of a hardening valve.
LUB SHHHHH DUB of an
incompetent one.
The gallop of
the failing
heart.

What if I were to lay you down, trusted interpreter? What might I hear if my ears were not filled with ossiculations of malleus, incus and stapes transposing tympanic rumblings from infarcting hearts? Rubs and rales and rhonchi of breath's malevolence. Pneumonia's crepitations.
Vocal fremitus. The turbulence of bruits. Tinkling from an obstructed bowel.
Borborygmi of an overactive one. My skull's vault reverberates,
echoing with this ceaseless cacophony,
an ensemble of bellowing wind.
Syncopated percussion.
The pizzicato
tugging of
strings.

What if I were to take you in hand again, wise counsel? Invite you to help me auscultate my own heart. Hippocratic secrets loiter within the unchartered caves of my atria and ventricles, darting between slaps from chordae tendineae and the recoiling of papillary muscles. Spectres haunt this myocardial cathedral, a choral curtain shrouding its confessional confines. Could you
open my ears to the beauty within those soulful songs? And guide me
to hear them as hymns. Not laments. May I too pray for
absolution? Release from responsibility.
So that I may lay down with
you. And rest.
Finally
rest.

SPEED GRIEVING

After Elisabeth Kübler-Ross and Samuel Shem

I
PTSD
me?
no way
no fucking way

II
I'm the doctor not the patient
I do all that burnout prevention shit
diet
exercise
meditation
I even got a hobby for god's sake
and here I am being told I've got PTSD
haven't I always taught my students how to stay sane
like *at a cardiac arrest take your own pulse first*
and *always remember the patient is the one with the disease*
no this can't be happening to me

III
it's all their fault
my patients don't do what I tell them
the receptionists keep fitting in all those extras

ONE CURIOUS DOCTOR

medicare doesn't pay me what I'm worth
the hospitals never communicate with me
they're all trying to kill me
bastards

IV
if I try harder
eat better
exercise more
drink less
work more to reduce my waiting list
work less to have more time off
take a holiday
then will my problems magically disappear?
if I'm good can You make this happen?

V
I can't see the point
I've tried everything
nothing works
I still feel like shit
I still dread going to work
I still worry that my patients will die on me
it's hopeless

VI
something's gotta change
I can't keep going like this
the neck pain
the rashes
the insomnia
my body's telling me something
what'll it take for me to start listening?
yesterday I was a doctor
what am I now?

SPEED GRIEVING

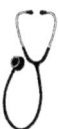

VII
I will be a patient
a good patient
because my job now
is to get better.

AFTER ALL THIS

My doctor sits back and with calm clarity tells me, 'You're done.'

'Done? What do you mean, done?'

'You've got PTSD. Classic case. An accumulation of forty-something years in medicine. All that vicarious trauma. The only safe solution is to stop work.'

I take this in, the message my body has been trying to give me for months. 'We're one doctor short for a couple of weeks. Can I work until next Friday and then take some time off?'

'No, you're done. You need to make that call.'

After this ...
I'm stuck sitting on the fence. I've got my left foot on one side of the pickets. *Should I be a good patient and do what my doctor says?* While my right foot is on the other side. *I'll be right. I'm not really that bad, am I?* The pickets are poking me right where it hurts. I spend an uncomfortable evening trying to decide what to do.

I decide to be a good patient. This is not easy for a doctor who thinks he always knows best. I phone my practice manager. 'I can't come into work. My doctor has advised extended leave. I don't know when I'll be able to return. Sorry to be such a nuisance.'

After this ...
I am surprised at how quickly I start to feel better after making the call. Within minutes, I feel a load lifting. *Have I been carrying*

this burden for all these years without realising? I thought I had good self-awareness.

After this …
My embarrassment and shame linger much longer than the weight on my shoulders. *I've let my patients down. I've let my colleagues down.* But having the weight off my shoulders is such a relief. *I wonder if my neck pain might disappear soon too?*

After this …
My identity takes a punch in the guts. *If I am not a doctor, what am I?* It's a relief to be able to continue my work as a teacher. *Doesn't the word 'doctor' mean 'teacher' anyway?*

After this …
Two of my soccer teammates are patients of mine. I phone them to explain why I am no longer able to be their doctor. I feel obligated to give them an explanation. I wonder how my sudden retirement will be for the rest of my patients. I ask the practice manager to let them know that I can't work because of health issues, but I don't know what the patients are actually told.

After this …
I feel bad that stopping work so abruptly didn't allow me the chance to say goodbye to my patients. On the other hand, if it had been a planned retirement, weeks or months of repeating farewells would have been overwhelming.

After this …
I cross the road to avoid having to talk to one of my former patients. It feels wrong to do this, but better than having to explain myself. My situation. Especially when I don't fully understand it myself.

After this …
I miss being a doctor. I miss my patients. Mostly I miss the

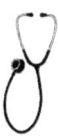

opportunity to be present with another human being. I don't miss having to fix insoluble problems. I don't miss having to get things right 100 per cent of the time. I don't miss constantly worrying about what might happen next. My life feels like it's teetering on a set of old-fashioned scales, like the ones used by the post office to weigh the mail. All I can do is hope that what I don't miss will eventually outweigh what I do miss.

After this ...

I begin to accept that my job now is to get better. And that it's a full-time job. I move more. I get up before dawn to walk over the headland. Sometimes I walk for a couple of hours. I have time to do this now. I eat less. I have the headspace to welcome hunger as a sign of being alive rather than an annoyance to instantly quell. After years of trying, I get my weight down to the healthy weight range.

After this ...

One of the practice owners phones me. 'Hilton, we've been holding your room for you in case you might be able to come back to work. Another doctor has approached us to work here. Do you think you will be returning, or can we give her your room?' I give up my room. Another bond severed.

After this ...

I retire from playing soccer. I've played for over fifty years, but it's too hard on my body now. Quitting is the sensible decision, but I miss playing. *What will be the next thing I love that I'm going to have to give up?*

After this ...

COVID hits just as I am starting to feel comfortable with no longer working as a GP. The guilt returns. I contact my old clinic and ask if I can help. Maybe some phone triage? They decline this offer. *Do they think I'm not capable?* I stop short of offering to return to clinical work. *I know I can't do that. My recurrent nightmares keep reminding me of this.*

After this ...

I run into one of my former chronically ill patients. I'd cared for her for more than twenty years. She followed me whenever I changed practices and continued to see me after she relocated an hour to the south. She now makes this drive to visit a new doctor. 'I miss you,' she says quietly after an uncomfortable greeting. 'Thanks,' I say. 'I had to stop work because of medical issues.' It's the best I can offer. It didn't seem right to say that I missed her too. 'Well, I hope that whatever you've got, it gets better soon,' she says with what appears to be genuine compassion. *Have our roles just reversed?*

After this ...

It's taken months, but I finally feel strong enough to clean out my room at the clinic. I sneak in the back door one Saturday morning to avoid being seen by people in the waiting room. It's weird seeing my room set up as someone else's room. Twenty years of medical possessions are packed in an old banana box in the corner. I return my keys to the receptionist and retreat, box in arms, tail between my legs.

After this ...

One morning I wake and realise that I haven't had neck pain for a few days. After three years of disturbed sleep, the need to take regular medications, and the discomfort of constant pain, it seems to have left me. I had hoped that it would disappear as soon as I stopped work. I guess it took years to build up, so it was going to take some time and a significant change in life habits to disappear. I realise now how I'd never fully understood why my patients were so keen to be free from pain. It's an indescribable relief.

After this ...

A piece I wrote about my journey into PTSD is published. I'm contacted by many doctors to thank me for my honesty. 'I thought I was the only one who felt like this.' 'Your writing made me cry. In a

AFTER ALL THIS

good way!' 'Thank you, Hilton, for giving me permission to take care of myself.' Maybe I am still doing what a doctor is meant to do.

After this ...
I expand my education roles to fill gaps left after stopping clinical work. I am learning how to ensure my teaching commitments do not encroach on the other things I love in life. Neck pain is now my ally rather than the enemy it was for so many years. It tells me when I need to pull my head in! Maybe it was trying to be an ally all along.

After this ...
I join the local walking football club. It's good exercise. It's social. It's the perfect pace for me. My footballing strengths – control the ball, head up, pass – finally outweigh my deficiencies – lack of speed, inability to dribble past players, reluctance to go in for heavy tackle. There's no white line fever. I love it.

After this ...
When I speak at conferences now, I introduce myself as a GP *from* Lennox Head. In the past, I'd say that I was a GP *in* Lennox Head. The power of a change in a preposition! It helps me feel that I am not being deceitful if I don't disclose that I am no longer seeing patients.

After this ...
At our local gallery, I see a woman making hand-carved wooden spoons. It piques my interest. She tells me where she learnt. Despite my fears – *I've never made anything with my hands before, I'll be no good at this* – I enrol in a one-day class. It's so different to anything I've done before. It's about taking away and seeing what emerges. I love it.

After this ...
I'm having a weekday brunch with my wife at a local café. The chef is a former patient of mine. I see him as I'm paying the bill and thank him for a delicious meal. 'Thanks for that, Hilton.' There's an awkward pause. I sense he wants to say more. 'And thanks for

everything you did for me over the years. You were a great doctor. I miss you.' I finally realise how I can respond to these acts of gratitude. 'Thanks, I miss our conversations too.' *Conversations* feels so much safer than *you*. Especially when talking with a middle-aged man.

After this ...
A mate builds me a workbench in our backyard. It's my spoon-carving spot. I use branches from our citrus and native trees to make oddly shaped spoons. Time disappears as the spoons emerge.

After this ...
I subscribe to *New Philosopher* magazine and read an article each morning with breakfast. My new rule is not to look at my phone until I've read something that supports my brain and my spirit. It's so much more nourishing to read about uncertainty, love, truth or identity than starting my day with the latest COVID stats.

After this ...
I've become a compost king. Our vegetable garden flourishes. I plant a food forest under our citrus trees. Sweet potato. Jalapeños. Basil. Cucumber. Ginger. Turmeric. We grow more than we can eat. I've become a pickling prince.

After this ...
I used to have a recurring dream that I was about to sit my final exams at medical school. I don't feel adequately prepared and panic that I will fail my exam. I always wake from this dream with the same question. *How could I be so stupid to put myself in this position?* My recurring dream has changed. Now I dream that I am back working as a doctor. I don't feel adequately prepared and panic that I will fail my patients. I wake from this dream with the same question. *How could I be so stupid to put myself in this position again?*

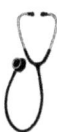

After this …

The more I write about my experiences over the last few years, the better I feel. Some of the pieces are published. It seems that my writing has an impact. Maybe sharing my story can help other people to feel better too.

And after all this …

Here we sit. You, and this one curious doctor. Sharing stories. What could be more healing than that?

PS

One Curious Doctor is an amalgam of pieces written over the last twelve years. Its conception, gestation and birth was a journey of discovery. I've been fortunate to have many fellow explorers join me.

My patients have been my greatest teachers. They have been the making of me. My heart glowed with gratitude at the generosity of the former patients I contacted to ask permission to share their story, or that of a deceased relative. They seemed equally touched that I thought their stories worth sharing. Those stories are the bones of this book.

While I've had no formal training in writing, I have been expertly supported and encouraged along the way. Kelly DuMar, who I met through a Transformative Language Arts Network course, and Kim Suhr from Red Oak Writing, have guided my development and helped me believe in myself as a writer.

My dear friend, colleague and mentor Frank Meumann has nurtured my love for imagination and metaphor. My other writing buddies, Jenny Bird and Michael Brown, have read drafts way before they should ever have seen the light of day.

Some of the pieces in this book have had a previous life, often under different titles, in publications willing to support an emerging writer from rural Australia. I am grateful for the support of these journals:

PS

The Examined Life Journal (Bearing Witness, What If I'd Listened to My Heart)

Pulse (The Making of Me, Wanderings, I Remember You)

Grieve (How Many Patients Can I See in One House Call, I'm Losing My Patients, Denial Impossible)

Hektoen International (Ode to My Stethoscope)

Please See Me (Diary of a ~~Wimpy~~ Wounded Doc)

Snapdragon (After the Funeral, The Medicine of Presence)

Dreamer's Creative (Black Dog Stew)

The Journal of Expressive Writing (Speed Grieving)

The Write Launch (Ignoring Vital Signs)

I thought the hard part of writing a book was going to be the writing. I was wrong. The greatest challenge has been pulling these disparate pieces into some form of collective whole. I've been blessed to be guided by the wisdom, humanity and expertise of Mish Phillips and Ben Phillips from Hambone Publishing. Thank you for your patience and your willingness to experiment with my crazy off-grid ideas.

Much of the hard work in writing this book was done during a number of Alumni Residencies at Varuna, The Writers' House, in Katoomba. I am grateful for the space provided and for the encouragement and support of Varuna staff and other writers during my stays.

The essence of *One Curious Doctor* is how family shapes us. My immediate family has shaped me in so many remarkable ways. My response to their loving support? Asking them to read my work in its formative stages! Their feedback has been invaluable in its raw honesty. I can't thank you enough Sharon, Liam and Aliza.

And finally, thanks to you, the readers of *One Curious Doctor*. These stories are in your care now. I wish them (and you) a long life.

Wakefield Press is an independent publishing and
distribution company based in Adelaide, South Australia.
We love good stories and publish beautiful books.
To see our full range of books, please visit our website at
www.wakefieldpress.com.au
where all titles are available for purchase.
To keep up with our latest releases, news and events,
subscribe to our monthly newsletter.

Find us!

Facebook: www.facebook.com/wakefield.press
Twitter: www.twitter.com/wakefieldpress
Instagram: www.instagram.com/wakefieldpress

www.ingramcontent.com/pod-product-compliance
Lightning Source LLC
Chambersburg PA
CBHW061246230426
43662CB00021B/2445